c|net Do-It-Yourself Windows Vista™ PROJECTS

24 cool things you didn't know you could do!

Curt Simmons

McGraw Hill

New York   Chicago   San Francisco
Lisbon   London   Madrid   Mexico City
Milan   New Delhi   San Juan
Seoul   Singapore   Sydney   Toronto

The McGraw-Hill Companies

Cataloging-in-Publication Data is on file with the Library of Congress

McGraw-Hill books are available at special quantity discounts to use as premiums and sales promotions, or for use in corporate training programs. For more information, please write to the Director of Special Sales, Professional Publishing, McGraw-Hill, Two Penn Plaza, New York, NY 10121-2298. Or contact your local bookstore.

CNET Do-It-Yourself Windows Vista™ Projects: 24 Cool Things You Didn't Know You Could Do!

1234567890 QPD QPD 01987

ISBN-13: 978-0-07-148561-6
ISBN-10: 0-07-148561-9

Sponsoring Editor
Roger Stewart

Editorial Supervisor
Janet Walden

Project Manager
Vasundhara Sawhney

Acquisitions Coordinator
Carly Stapleton

Copy Editor
Lisa McCoy

Proofreader
Benodini Banerjei

Indexer
Stephen Ingle

Production Supervisor
Jean Bodeaux

Composition
International Typesetting and Composition

Illustration
International Typesetting and Composition

Art Director, Cover
Jeff Weeks

Cover Illustration
Sarah Howell

Cover Icons
VistaICO.com

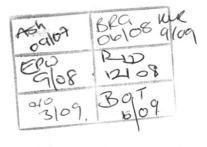
This book is for Mattie, with love.

About the Author

Curt Simmons is a technology author and trainer with a focus on Microsoft products. He is the author of more than 50 general technology books on a wide variety of subjects, including Windows, Microsoft Office, IT certification titles, networking, and many more. When he is not teaching or writing, he spends his time with his wife and children and constantly working on his 107-year-old Victorian home. His latest book, *How to Do Everything with Windows Vista*, is also available from McGraw-Hill/Osborne.

Contents

Foreword

The PC is the foundation of today's digital lifestyle, and Windows is the foundation for the PC. Riding on its shoulders are the Web, e-mail, digital photography, music and video, podcasts, our finances, and, yes, Solitaire.

Windows Vista is the latest iteration of the operating system that has loomed large for 15 years. It benefits greatly from those miles on the road, and from a lot of knocks taken along the way. It no longer deserves the tired clichés about blue screens and crashes, and it's the stage for the largest assortment of great software and hardware in the world of computing.

This is not to say that the various versions of Vista are perfect. The Achilles heel of any powerful operating system is complexity—it does a lot, so you have to learn a lot, no way around that. That's where this book steps in, with concise lessons on two dozen delightful capabilities of Vista that you might miss in cursory look around the Desktop.

Many of our insider secrets deal with media, from watching TV on your Vista machine to creating your own digital movies. Most versions of Vista include Media Center, and we show you how to join the living room revolution by using Vista as a killer home entertainment system. And while housekeeping such as backups and lost file retrieval glaze the eyes of many users, the fact that you have picked up this book suggests you'll value those chapters as much as I do.

An operating system like Windows Vista is not an end in itself. It creates an environment to do things both productive and entertaining. If you utilize the projects in this book, you'll enjoy doing a lot more of both.

Brian Cooley
CNET Editor-at-Large

Acknowledgments

I would like to thank the many folks at McGraw-Hill/Osborne and CNET for making this book a reality. Thanks to Roger Stewart for giving me the green light, Carly Stapleton for keeping things moving in the right direction, Lisa McCoy for the eagle eye, and Vasundhara Sawhney for bringing it all together. I would also like to thank my agent, Margot, for her support.

Introduction

You waited a long time for a new Microsoft operating system. Sure, Windows XP was nice, but you wanted something more...something smarter, more suave, and more useful. Hopefully, you've found it in Windows Vista, the latest offering from Microsoft.

Windows Vista is a power-packed, intricate operating system. It does more than previous versions of Windows and can be used in many different ways. Fortunately, if you've used Windows XP, you can probably find your way around, at least initially. But there's a lot more you probably didn't know you could do.

That's why this book is in your hands. You want to do more with Windows Vista, and you want to do it yourself, right from the comfort of home. With this book, you can do just that.

What You'll Do

This book consists of 24 separate projects, divided into three categories: Easy Projects, Challenging Projects, and Advanced Projects. Here are examples of what you'll find:

- **Easy Projects** Finding stuff in Windows Vista, have Web content delivered to you, create a personal sidebar, customize folders and flip action, use tabbed browsing, use Windows collaboration, arrange and view photos and slide shows, and manage parental controls.

- **Challenging Projects** Create custom CD covers and movies, use Windows Vista as a media center, watch and record TV on Windows Vista, talk to Windows Vista, synchronize Windows Vista with other devices, and eliminate spam and junk e-mail.

- **Advanced Projects** Improve your computer's performance, back up your computer and important data, use a network map, retrieve lost files with shadow copy, use Windows Meeting Space, and find your way around using GPS on Windows Vista.

Each project is a self-contained series of steps that take you from point A to point B. Feel free to work through these projects in order, or just skip around and tackle the projects you're really interested in first. Each project begins by telling you what you'll need and if there is any additional cost or things to buy first. In most cases, you already have everything you need built right into Windows Vista.

Conventions Used in This Book

To make things easier for you, this book uses various conventions, with three I specifically want to mention here:

- Note, Tip, and Caution paragraphs highlight important information. Make sure you pay attention to these items.

- The pipe character or vertical bar (|) denotes a step-by-step action to get to some place in Windows Vista. For example, when I say click Start | Control Panel, I mean to click the Start button to open the menu, and then click the Control Panel option on the Start menu. Use the keyboard, mouse, or a combination of the two if you wish.

- Most check boxes have two states: selected (with a check mark in them) and cleared (without a check mark in them). This book tells you to select a check box or clear a check box rather than "click to place a check mark in the box" or "click to remove a check mark from the box." This convention makes the book faster and easier to read.

Part I

Easy

Project 1

Quickly Find Anything on Your Computer

What You'll Need

- Windows Vista: Any version
- Cost: Free

When you break it all down, a computer is a storehouse of information. After all, one of the reasons you have parted with your hard-earned money and bought a computer is to create and keep information. From documents to photos to music, your computer is designed to keep up with your life.

That's good news for me. As a writer and teacher, I am constantly creating documents and files, but I also have an affinity for digital photography and I'm a music lover as well. As you can imagine, it doesn't take me long to crowd my computer with information. Yet, as organized as I am, I have a tendency to lose information within the computer. A file gets neglected or put in the wrong place, and then I have no idea where it is.

Since Microsoft Windows Vista is essentially organized by folders where you store information, you have to keep track of where that information is stored. The good news is that Windows Vista can help you quickly locate any file or data on your computer.

Step 1: Get to Know Windows Vista Folders

Your computer works like a filing cabinet. Folders are used to hold documents and information, but folders can also hold other folders. You can use some default folders that you find on the Start menu—Documents, Pictures, Music, and Games—and you can also create your own folders anywhere you like. For example, within the Pictures folder on my computer, I have photos, but I have also created other folders in there to store certain groupings of photos.

If you open a folder, you'll notice right away that the appearance of folders in Windows Vista is different from earlier versions of Windows. Don't worry—this is good news for you because the new folder features make managing your information easier.

When you open a folder, you'll several important items that are explained in the following list and shown in Figure 1-1:

- **Address bar**   Identifies the folder you are in.

- **Search box**   Type a name to look for a file here

- **Favorite links**   This area simply gives you access to other folders within Windows Vista.

- **Folders**   The area shows a folder structure, which highlights the folder you are in. You can jump to another folder from here as well.

- **File list**   This area shows you what files and other folders are found in the folder.

- **Details pane**   Select a file to find out details about it here.

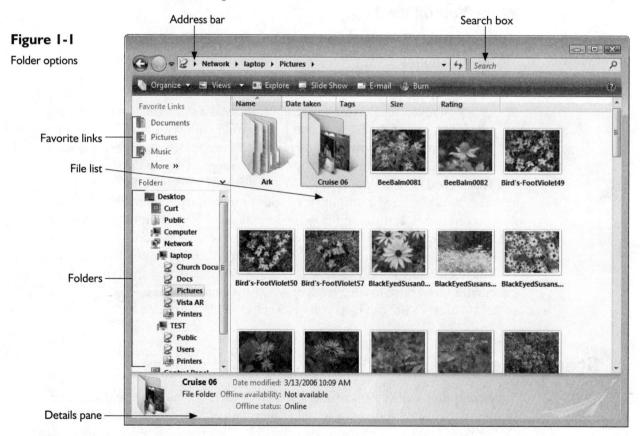

Figure 1-1
Folder options

Create a New Folder

In order to keep things organized, you'll need to create sub-folders from time to time. Sub-folders reside under an existing folder. For example, if you create additional folders in the Pictures folder, those folders are called sub-folders. You can quickly create new folders (or sub-folders) and place files in them as needed.

I. In any folder, click Organize | New Folder, as shown in the following illustration.

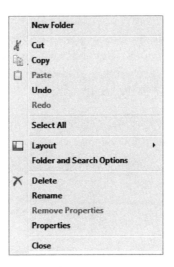

2. The new folder appears in the file list, as shown in the following illustration. Its name will be highlighted so that you can type a new name. Simply start typing the new name, and then press ENTER.

3. You can now begin dragging files to the folder in order to store them there.

tip *Do you want a new folder on your desktop? Simply right-click the desktop, and click New | Folder.*

Adjust the File List

As you look at a folder, you may notice that the File list is simply a listing of files by name. That's fine as it is, but depending on the kind of file you're looking for, you may want to quickly adjust the size of the File list. For example, notice the following two illustrations. The first contains only a listing of the file names. However, since these items are photos, it is easier to find what I want by increasing the view size so that I can actually see the photos instead of just the file names.

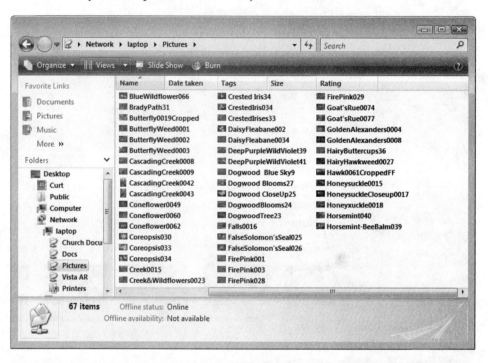

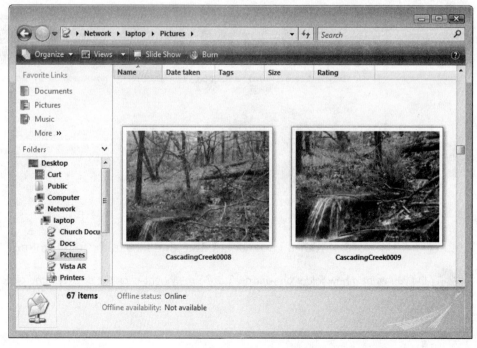

The good news is that you can adjust the size of the file icons in a folder at any time. Simply click the Views option on the toolbar. You'll see a slider bar option appear, where you can change the view of the icons from a simple list all the way up to large icons.

Step 2: Turn On the Preview Pane

As you're looking for items within folders, Windows Vista has a new feature that helps you quickly find the item that you want. It's called the Preview pane, and it is especially helpful with documents and spreadsheets. Because the name of a document or spreadsheet could be a bit of mystery to you, the Preview pane gives you a preview of the file without your having to open it. This feature enables you to click through items in the folder and see a quick preview without having to actually open the file.

To display the Preview pane, click Organize | Layout | Preview Pane. As you can see in Figure 1-2, the Preview pane displays the contents of the selected file.

Figure 1-2

The Preview pane displays the contents of a file.

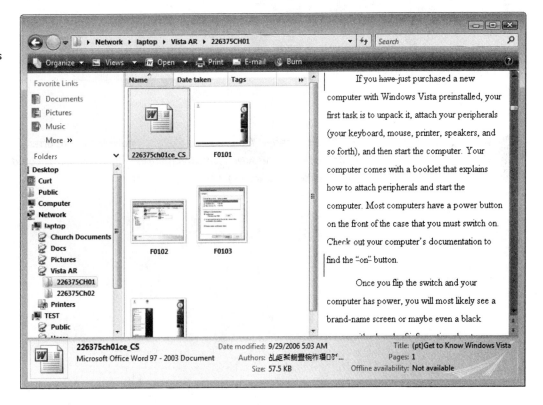

Step 3: Search in a Folder

In every Windows folder, a search box appears in the upper-left corner. When you type a name or word in the search box, Windows filters what you see in the folder based on your search. The search filter looks for the words you typed in file names, tags you've applied to files, in the files' properties, and even within the contents of files. Simply type the name, part of the name, or even a keyword in the search box, and you'll see the File list within the folder change to show your top matches. If you don't find what you're looking for within the folder, try a different search.

When you search, you'll see "Did you find what you were searching for?" in the File list, with an option for Advanced Search. If you click the Advanced Search option, your folder will change to provide additional search boxes for location, date, size, file name, tags, and even the author of the file, as you can see in Figure 1-3. These features can help you be more specific in your search. The Advanced Search is especially helpful with folders that have a lot of data that is similar in nature (such as a folder containing 50 Word documents that are all related to your business or to a certain project).

Figure 1-3

Advanced search options

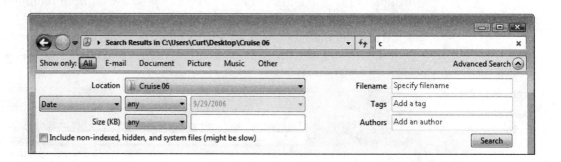

tip   *Keep your search as simple as possible. You are more likely to find what you're after if you don't supply every piece of information in the Advanced Search boxes. The more complicated your search parameters, the less likely you are to find what you want.*

Step 4: Search in All Folders

So you wrote an invoice in Microsoft Excel and you stored it in the correct folder, or so you thought. Now, however, you have searched the folder and the invoice obviously isn't there. You know it is somewhere on your computer, but you have no idea where. No problem—you can perform a global search that will look in every folder on your computer.

To start a global search, click the Start button. You'll see a Start Search box at the bottom of the Start menu, shown in the following illustration.

As you being typing the criteria on which you want to search, the Start menu contents will change to hopefully help you find what you're after, as shown in the following illustration. If not, click the Search Everywhere option, and a new folder appears that will search through all of your folders to find what you're after. Also notice that you can search the Internet as well by clicking the Search The Internet option on the

Start menu. This action opens Microsoft Internet Explorer, taking you to Microsoft's search site, www.live.com.

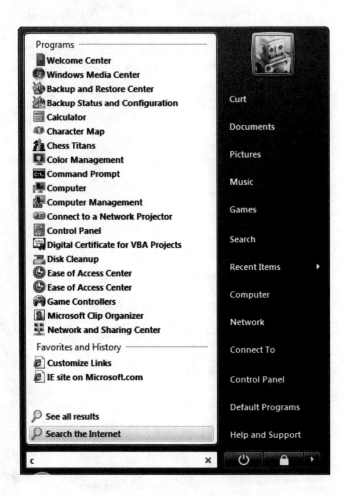

Project 2

Use the Internet Better with Live Tools and Services

What You'll Need

- **Windows Vista: Any version**
- **An Internet connection**
- **Cost: Free**

About the time Windows Vista was getting ready to release, Microsoft also entered the Web service arena with a new Web site called Windows Live, found at www.live.com. If you visit the Web site, you may think that Windows Live is just a search engine. While this service is offered, the site also provides many other services and tools that give you a much more integrated and fun Web experience. In fact, one of the tools can even help keep your PC safe while you're connected to the Internet.

In this project, I want to give you a quick overview of the services that you can find with Windows Live, and then I want to especially look at the Windows Live toolbar and Windows Live OneCare. So get connected to the Internet and let's have fun!

Step 1: Visit Windows Live

If you click Start | All Programs | Accessories | Welcome Center, you can see some of the options that are provided for you with Windows Live in the Offers From Microsoft section of this window, shown in Figure 2-1. At the time of this writing, some of the Windows Live services are still under development, so the offers you see on the Welcome Center may vary a bit from those you see here. Nevertheless, the Welcome Center is one way to begin accessing Windows Live services.

Figure 2-1

Welcome Center

Aside from the Welcome Center, you can also check out the services at http:// get.live.com, shown in Figure 2-2. On the Windows Live site, you can click the different service options and learn more about them. Here's a quick review of what's available at the time of this writing (you may see more options, which is a good thing!):

Figure 2-2

Windows Live toolbar

- **Live Search**   This option enables you to search the Web. You can find the basic search feature at www.live.com, but you can also get maps, directions, and other local information at www.local.live.com. You can increase your interactivity with the Web by using the Windows Live toolbar, which we'll explore later in this project.

- **Live.com**   This default page gives you a place to personalize Web searches and even add gadgets for fun and interactivity. You can save your searches and even access Really Simple Syndication (RSS) content feeds. It's a great way to create a personalized Web search portal.

- **Windows Live Expo**   Use this service to buy, sell, and communicate with people you trust. You can sell items through the Live Expo via Windows Live

Spaces and Windows Live Messenger, post an ad for free and even control who sees it, or you can browse other items that are for sale.

● **Windows Live Messenger** Windows Live Messenger replaces the older MSN Messenger. It gives you the ability to send text messages; call your friends' phones or PCs; use full-screen, full-motion video calling; share your photos and folders; and more. The following illustration gives you an initial look at Windows Live Messenger.

● **Windows Live Mail** Windows Live Mail is a Web mail client. It is fast and easy, with drag-and-drop capability, preview options, 2 gigabytes (GB) of storage, junk e-mail filters, and more. The following illustration shows you an example of the Windows Mail Client.

- **Windows Live Spaces** Use the Windows Live Spaces option to create your own blog in minutes. You can add up to 500 photos a month, choose a layout and colors, network with your friends, and update your blog from almost any mobile device that can send e-mail.

- **Windows Live OneCare** Windows Live OneCare is a new set of services designed to help keep your PC safe while you're on the Internet. We'll explore the OneCare options later in this project.

- **More Options** At the time of this writing, other services are also in development, such as Windows Live Favorites (Web favorites at home or on the go), Windows Live Alerts (traffic, news, stocks, etc.), Windows Live Custom Domains (free e-mail for your Internet domain), and Windows Live for mobile devices.

Step 2: Use the Windows Live Toolbar

One of the Windows Live features that gives you more interactivity with the Internet from your PC is the Windows Live toolbar. You can download the toolbar and install it on your PC by accessing the Welcome Center or http://get.live.com.

The Windows Live toolbar appears in Microsoft Internet Explorer once the installation to your computer is complete. The first time you open Internet Explorer after installing the toolbar, you will see it displayed as shown in Figure 2-2.

Customize the Toolbar

As you can see, the toolbar offers you several important features that can help you when surfing the Web. First things first, if you click the See More Options button (the first one on the toolbar), you can access a few basic features as well as the Toolbar Options area, shown in Figure 2-3. In the Display area, you can determine what toolbar buttons appear on the toolbar. Simply clear the relevant check boxes to remove buttons that you don't want. In the left pane, you have different options for the display, install and remove buttons, Web search options, and general features. These items are self-explanatory: Just select each one to see how you can customize the toolbar to meet your needs.

Figure 2-3

Windows Live toolbar options

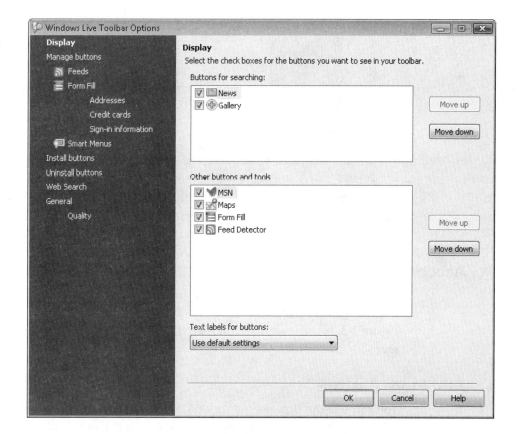

Use the Search Options

The Windows Live toolbar contains a cool search feature. You can see it as a search box on the toolbar. So what's cool about that? If you click the drop-down menu next to the toolbar, you can narrow the search so it's more specific. For example, in Figure 2-4, I am searching for "cats." However, if I click the drop-down menu, I can narrow my search instantly by performing a Web search, news search, local information search, images, feeds, or even my e-mail, documents, and pictures for "cats." This way, I find exactly what I want more quickly.

Figure 2-4

Use the drop-down menu to narrow your search.

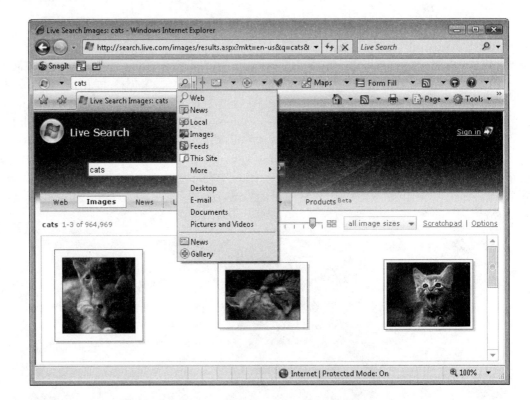

In addition, you have default buttons to search news on MSNBC or you can search the MSN site for additional items. Naturally, Microsoft puts MSN options on the toolbar, but remember that you can remove these buttons if you prefer not to use them.

Access Maps

Another good feature of the toolbar is the maps feature. The Maps button takes you to Live Local, where you can enter a search location and see a map to it, shown in Figure 2-5. Notice that you can search for businesses or people and can access general maps for cities and towns.

Add More Buttons

You can use the Buttons option on the toolbar to access Windows Live and see what additional buttons can be added to the toolbar. You'll find many options, and more

Figure 2-5

Live Local options

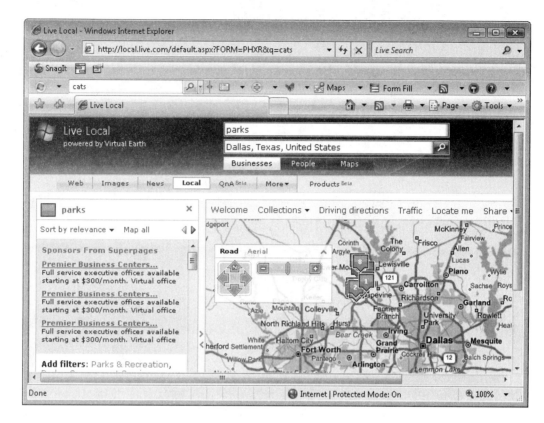

are constantly being added. If you like to keep track of the weather, consider adding the Weather button to get instant weather updates. You'll also find buttons for MSN Movies, Amazon.com, Wikipedia, and more. Explore the buttons available so that you can truly get the toolbar options you want.

Use Form Fill

Do you get tired of entering the same information over and over? With the Form Fill feature, you can instantly enter your address, credit card information, or sign-in information. Your data is secure, but when you encounter a Web form that needs this information, just have Form Fill complete the form for you. No more redundant typing!

Step 3: Use Windows Live OneCare

Windows Live OneCare is a service that provides firewall, antivirus, antispyware, back-ups and even tune-ups for your system. It's automatic, self-updating, and can even scan your system to see what needs to be done to your PC. This service can be very helpful because as long as your PC is on and connected to the Internet, OneCare is also on and running. Think of it as a permanent security guard for your PC.

You can download the OneCare features from http://get.live.com and try it out for free. OneCare works with both Windows XP and Windows Vista operating systems, and once you install it, you have the opportunity to review it for 90 days before you decide to subscribe to the service.

Project 3

Create a Personal Windows Sidebar

What You'll Need

- Windows Vista: Any version
- An Internet connection
- Cost: Free

One of the new features you'll see immediately in Windows Vista is the Windows Sidebar. The Sidebar is the strip you see running along the right side of your desktop. It probably came to you configured with some default icons and not much else. Maybe you thought, "This is neat... sort of." At first glance, you may not realize that the Sidebar can hold all kinds of live icons, as well as some basic tools that you'll use over and over again. The good news is that the Sidebar is customizable: You can make it hold all kinds of things that are useful to you, and you can make it look and behave the way you want it to.

Step 1: Adjust the Basic Behavior of the Sidebar

Before you start adding content to the Sidebar, it's a good idea to first configure it so that the Sidebar looks and behaves the way you want. Windows Vista makes it easy to make basic changes to it.

Get Familiar with the Sidebar

The Windows Sidebar, shown in Figure 3-1, gives you easy access to Windows Live icons, as well as basic tools that you tend to use over and over again. For example, I like keeping a calculator on the Sidebar because this is a basic tool that I use all of the time.

Figure 3-1

The Windows Sidebar
is the long vertical bar
you see when you start
Windows.

By default, the Sidebar appears on the right side of your screen and it always starts up whenever you start Windows. When you work with Windows Vista, other windows can cover up the sidebar by default, but this is a behavior that you can change (as you'll see in the next section).

The sidebar holds mini-programs that are called gadgets. Gadgets are designed to offer information or provide some kind of tool, such as in the case of the calculator. The idea behind the Sidebar is to configure it in such a way that it holds the gadgets that are most useful to you. With the Sidebar, you can keep the most needed information directly on your desktop at all times.

Changing the Sidebar's Basic Behavior

In addition to customizing the gadgets you want displayed, you can customize the Sidebar by changing its basic properties. Click Start | Control Panel | Windows Sidebar. You'll see the Windows Sidebar Properties dialog box appear, shown in

Figure 3-2

Taskbar and Start
menu properties

Figure 3-2. You can also access this dialog box by right-clicking an empty area of the Sidebar and clicking Properties.

You have the following options:

- **Sidebar Is Always On Top Of Other Windows**   This option always keeps the Sidebar on top of any window that is open. This feature is good in that it keeps the Sidebar content visible to you, but you may find that it gets in the way as you work with Windows Vista and other programs, depending on the size of your monitor. The good news is that you can try this setting and always change it back if you don't like it. Click the check box to enable it.

- **Start Sidebar When Windows Starts**   This option is enabled by default and is typically the best setting because you'll see your Sidebar content as soon as you start Windows. If you don't want the Sidebar to start when Windows starts, however, just clear the check box.

- **Start Sidebar On This Side Of The Screen**   By default, the sidebar starts on the right side of the screen (the Right option is selected by default), but you can select the Left option instead. Notice that the sidebar is a not an old-style Windows toolbar. You can't drag it around the screen: It either resides on the right or left side, depending on your choice here.

- **Start Sidebar On This Monitor**   This option is useful for people who are using a multiple-monitor configuration. The default setting is 1 because Windows Vista assumes that you're using one monitor. However, if you're using a multiple display, you can have the Sidebar appear on whichever monitor you prefer.

● **View Gadgets**   Click this button to see the gadgets that are currently on the Sidebar. You'll see an additional dialog box appear listing the gadgets, shown in Figure 3-3. You can select one and click the Remove button to remove it from the Sidebar. Note that removing a gadget from the Sidebar doesn't remove the gadget from your computer: You can always put the gadget back on the Sidebar later if you like.

Figure 3-3

Select a gadget and click Remove to remove it from the Sidebar.

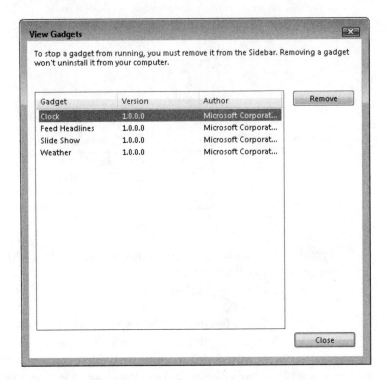

Step 2: Adding, Removing, and Detaching Gadgets

The Sidebar is all about the gadgets that you choose to use, so now the fun really begins! You can easily add, remove, and move gadgets on the Sidebar any time and in any way that you want. You can also download more gadgets from the Internet to your computer.

Add a Gadget to the Sidebar

You can easily add a gadget to the Sidebar at any time. If you right-click an empty area of the Sidebar and choose Add Gadgets, a window opens, listing all of the gadgets currently on your computer. You can also click the plus sign (+) toward the top of the Sidebar to open the gadgets window, as shown in the following illustration.

You can scroll through the gadgets and even search for one in particular using the Search dialog box. Notice that if you select a gadget, a short summary of what the gadget does appears in the bottom half of the window, as you can see in Figure 3-4.

Figure 3-4

Locate the gadget you want.

Once you've found the gadget that you want to add, drag it to the Sidebar using your mouse. The gadget will be added. You can also double-click a gadget to install it on the Sidebar.

> **tip**   *You can drag the gadget to any location on the Sidebar that you want. If you right-click a gadget, you'll notice a Move option. Use the Move feature if you can't drag a gadget to a new location on the Sidebar. Once you choose Move, you'll be able to move the gadget around as desired.*

Removing a Gadget

If you're like me, I tend to use gadgets for a period of time, but as my needs and wants change, I may remove some gadgets and add others. You can remove a gadget from the Sidebar at any time. This action doesn't remove the gadget from your computer—it simply removes it from the Sidebar. You can always return to the gadgets window and add the gadget again if you would like. To remove a gadget, simply right-click it and click Remove.

Detaching a Gadget from the Sidebar

Keep in mind that gadgets are mini-programs. Since this is the case, you may want to detach a gadget from the Sidebar and use it on your desktop for a period of time (or all of the time if you like). This is especially helpful for gadgets that you want to interact with. For example, in Figure 3-5, I have detached the weather gadget. Now it appears on my desktop in a larger version so that I can work with it more easily. Once I'm done, I can simply put it back on the Sidebar.

Figure 3-5

Detached gadgets are often larger and easier to work with.

To detach a gadget from the Sidebar, right-click the gadget and click Detach From Sidebar. You can reattach the gadget to the Sidebar by right-clicking it and clicking Attach To Sidebar or simply dragging it back to the Sidebar.

Step 3: Customize Gadgets

Some gadgets give you the ability to customize certain things about them, depending on the gadget. If you right-click a gadget on the Sidebar and see a Settings button, then that gadget has some customizable features you can explore. Since every gadget has its own setting options, we'll not explore each setting available (and besides, most of them are self-explanatory); however, let's take a look at the clock gadget as an example. As you can see in Figure 3-6, I have accessed the options for the clock.

Figure 3-6

Options for the clock gadget

The clock options let you choose a clock style by clicking through the selection arrows. You can then give the clock a name, choose your time zone, and decide if you want to show the second hand on the clock or not. Once you're done, click OK to apply your settings.

If you're using the slide show gadget, be sure and check out the settings. You can determine what photos (including your own) appear on the slide show, and you can choose how quickly the photos rotate and what transition is used.

Step 4: Find More Gadgets Online

A few gadgets are installed with Windows Vista by default. However, you can find additional gadgets on the Internet. If you right-click the Sidebar and click Add Gadgets, you will see the Get More Gadgets Online link. Clicking this will take you to the Windows Vista Gadgets gallery, as you can see in Figure 3-7. Here, you can scroll through the available gadgets, search for a particular gadget, and download any gadget that you want to your computer. You can then use it as you would any other gadget. You can also go to www.microsoftgadgets.com to find additional gadgets and download them as well.

Figure 3-7

Find more gadgets online.

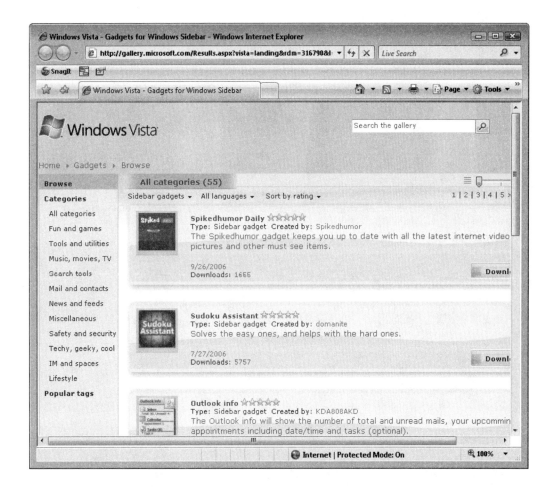

Project 4

Customize Folders and Flip Action

What You'll Need

- Windows Vista: Any version
- Cost: Free

In Windows Vista, a folder is simply a place to put something, typically a file of some kind. You may have files created for work purposes, or you may have photos, videos, and audio files. You may also have gaming files. In the end, a folder exists in Windows to help you store stuff and manage it well, and in today's computing environment, that's a good thing.

You may think, "Computer folders have been around forever; what's so special about Windows Vista?" In truth, folders in Windows Vista work the way they always have in Windows, but the folders you see in Windows Vista are customizable and designed to help you get your work done easier In fact, Windows Vista makes it easy for you to use several different folders at the same time. It's all about finding and using information. In this project, you'll see how to customize folders for this purpose and how to use Windows Vista's new flip action feature.

Step 1: Explore Folder Options

As you think about customizing folders in Windows Vista, your first stop is not even in a folder—it's in Folder Options, which is a Control Panel applet. Here, you'll be able to configure some global behaviors of your folders that may not even realize are possible. Click Start | Control Panel. Make sure that Classic View is selected, and then double-click Folder Options.

The Folder Options properties dialog box gives you three tabs where you can make some decisions about how you want your folders to look and behave. The next three sections explain these options.

General Tab

The General tab, shown in Figure 4-1, gives you three basic sections. In the Tasks section, you can show previews and filters or use Windows classic folders. If you're really into retro, then the classic option may be for you. When you choose this option, you lose some of the newer folder features in Windows Vista for an old-style Windows look. However, this is probably not what you want, since you likely want to take advantage of all that Windows Vista has to offer, so it's best to leave the preview and filters options selected.

Figure 4-1

General tab

In the Browse Folders section, you can choose to open each folder in the same window or open each folder in its own window. The first option keeps things from getting cluttered up when you're working with multiple folders. However, on the other hand, it can also make things more confusing, since every new opened folder appears in the same window. Make the decision that is best for you concerning how you use folders.

In the Click Items As Follows area, you can choose a single-click option to open items or the standard double-click feature. This option is purely a matter of choice, so choose the option that you prefer.

View Tab

The View tab contains several check boxes that determine how your folders look and how icons behave. Notice in Figure 4-2 that for each option, Windows tells you if the feature is turned on or off (and you can also tell by which check boxes are selected). Most of the options you see here are self-explanatory, so you can make changes as desired. You can always try options and see if you like then, and then return here later to make additional changes. If you make too many changes and get confused, click the Restore Defaults button to return everything back to the way it originally was.

Figure 4-2

View tab

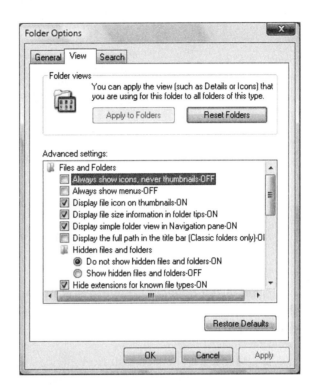

Search Tab

The Search tab, shown in Figure 4-3, enables you to configure how searches are performed in folders. In order to make data easier to find, all folders in Windows Vista have the search feature enabled by default. This tab allows you to determine how searches should be performed. The default options here are likely the best, because they search file names and contents in indexed locations as well as subfolders and partial matches. In other words, the default options will likely give you the best search results, so be sure to experiment with real searches before you change anything here.

Step 2: Choose Folder Layout

Windows Vista folders are essentially made up of different areas, or "panes," that give you some functionality within the folder. However, you can turn these different panes on or off by accessing the layout options, which enable you to choose a folder design that best fits your needs. You can also quickly change that design on the fly when necessary.

Figure 4-3

Search tab

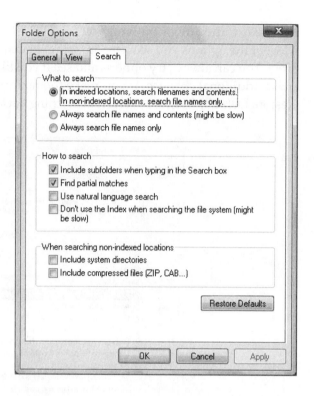

If you click Organize | Layout within a folder, you will see a menu of options, shown in Figure 4-4. Click the layout options to turn them on or off, depending on your needs:

- **Menu Bar**   When you first glance at a folder in Windows Vista, you might wonder what happened to standard menus, such as File, Edit, and so on. You'll now find them on the Organize menu, but if you want to put them back on the actual folder, click the Menu Bar option under Layout.

- **Search Pane**   The Search pane actually gives you an additional "bar," shown in the following illustration, where you can click the kind of file that you want to see or click to perform an advanced search. This pane is helpful when search-ing folders that have a lot of different kinds of data because you can narrow your search to just a specific kind of file with only the click of a button.

- **Details Pane**   The Details pane, shown in the following illustration, gives you information about the item that is currently selected. It appears at the bottom of your folder and can be helpful when you want quick details about a particular file.

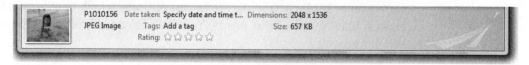

Figure 4-4

Layout options

● **Preview Pane**   The Preview pane appears on the right side of your folder, and it gives you a preview of a selected file. This feature works particular well with data files, such as a Microsoft Excel file or Microsoft Word document. Click the file and see a quick preview of the contents in the preview pane.

● **Navigation Pane**   The Navigation pane appears on the left side of your folder, and it contains links to common folders as well as to your folder structure, so you can quickly jump from one folder to another.

Step 3: Use Additional Customization Options

There is one other easily missed option that can give you some additional customization options. If you open a folder and click Organize | Properties, a Properties dialog box will appear with a Customize tab displayed, shown in Figure 4-5. You can choose a folder type for use as a template from the drop-down menu. For example, if your folder contains a mixture of items, you can choose the All Items option, or, if your folder contains mainly pictures and videos, you can choose that option as well. This feature helps Windows Vista understand the kinds of content you are working with so that the folder can give you additional items on the menu bar, such as Slide Show, Burn, Preview, E-mail, and so forth.

Figure 4-5

Customize options

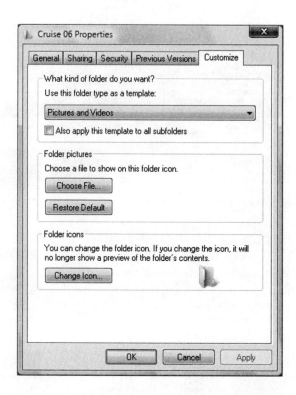

Also notice that you can choose a file to use as a picture, or icon, for the folder. This option enables you to show a picture on the folder icon so that you can more easily identify what's in the folder simply by looking at the picture. Click Choose File to choose the picture you want to use.

Step 4: Use Windows Flip 3D

Windows Vista includes a new graphical feature called Flip 3D that enables you to rotate through open folders quickly. Using this feature, you can quickly preview all open windows without having to click each one on the taskbar. With Flip 3D, your windows are displayed in a stack, and you can flip through the stack as you would a deck of cards, as shown in Figure 4-6.

To use Flip 3D, the Windows Aero feature must be turned on, which it is by default. To use Flip 3D, press the Windows logo key+TAB to open the feature. Then, while holding down the Windows logo key, press TAB repeatedly (or use the mouse wheel) to rotate through the cycle of currently open windows. You can also use the RIGHT ARROW or DOWN ARROW keys to cycle forward or use the LEFT ARROW and UP ARROW keys to cycle backward. Simple release the Windows logo key to display the frontmost window in the stack, or click any part of the window in the stack to display that window.

Figure 4-6

Flip 3D

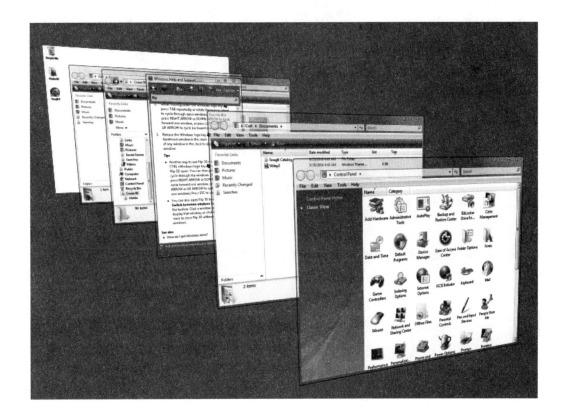

There are two other quick tricks that you may enjoy. You can turn on Flip 3D so that you don't have to hold down the Windows logo key by pressing CTRL+Windows logo+TAB. Now you can release the keys and simply press TAB or use the arrow keys to move through your windows.

Finally, if you want to quickly choose an open window, press CTRL+ALT+TAB. This gives you an option to view your open folders in a flat-screen look. Then use the TAB key to move through them and select the folder you want, as shown in Figure 4-7. All of these options make Windows easier to use and help you find what you want in a hurry.

Figure 4-7

Quick selection option

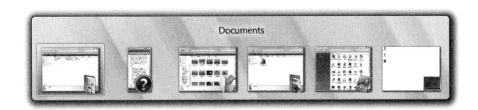

Project 5

Quickly Browse the Internet Using Tabs

What You'll Need

- **Windows Vista: Any version**
- **Cost: Free**

At this stage of the game, the Internet is nothing new, and Internet Explorer, Microsoft's Internet browser, is certainly nothing new. It seems like Internet Explorer has been around almost as long as Windows, and with each new Windows version, you get an updated Internet Explorer. In the past few years, changes to Internet Explorer have not been particularly impressive—new bells and whistles, but essentially the same old thing. The good news is that Internet Explorer 7, the new revision that comes to you with Windows Vista, has been redesigned in several ways. It's cleaner, easier to use, and includes a cool feature you're likely to overlook if you're not careful. However, this new feature can change the way you browse the Internet and make the Internet much friendlier to you. The feature? Tabbed browsing. Tabbed browsing lets you access several Web pages at the same time with a single mouse click. Intrigued? I thought so, and this project will show you how to use this new feature.

Step 1: Create Multiple Tabs

Let's say you're researching a topic. You've found seven Web sites with important information and you want to browse those sites. In the past, you had two options. You could add all of those sites your Favorites list as you found them, and then use the Favorites menu to switch between the sites; or you could open multiple Internet Explorer windows, minimizing and maximizing them as needed, which could be confusing and a real pain.

This is no longer the case. With tabbed browsing, you can see multiple Web sites in one Internet Explorer window. Each Web site that you want is "tabbed," and you simply flip through the tabs and look at Web sites much in the same way you would flip through file folders in a filing cabinet. It's fast, easy, and gives you a simple way to keep track of information you find on the Internet.

The first Web site you access after opening Internet Explorer is put on the first tab. As you can see in Figure 5-1, The MSN tab is located next to the Favorites buttons on the toolbar. If you look to the right of the tab, you'll see another, blank tab sitting behind it. If you point your mouse at this new tab, it will say "New Tab."

Figure 5-1

The first site sits on a tab, and the option to create a new tab resides next to it.

To add another tab, simply click the New Tab option (or press CTRL+T), and type the new address in the address bar. Now, as you can see in Figure 5-2, my browser has two tabs, MSN and Starwars.com. I can flip between the two sites just by clicking the tabs. You can add multiple tabs in this manner and then click the tabs to move between them.

Figure 5-2

Click the tabs to access the different sites.

However, what if you are browsing the Internet and you stumble across a link that you want to tab? Before clicking the link, right-click it and click Open In New Tab, shown in Figure 5-3. Or you can hold down the CTRL key and click the link, and it will be automatically opened in a new tab.

Figure 5-3

Right-click a link and choose to open it in a new tab.

If you end up with many tabs, you may find it difficult to click between them because it will be difficult to see all of the tabs' titles. No problem. Notice the little arrow to the left of the first tab. If you click this arrow, you'll see a drop-down menu of your current tabs so you can easily find the one you want.

Step 2: Closing Tabs

So you create five tabs as you are doing research on a topic. You find that one of the Web pages you have tabbed isn't that helpful, and you don't want to use it anymore. How do you close it? No problem. As you surf the Internet and create tabs for sites, you should close the tabs you no longer need in order to keep the number of tabs from getting out of control. Fortunately, this is quick and easy.

If you click a particular tab that you no longer want to use, you'll see the tab's name highlighted and a Close button appear on the tab (a red X), shown in Figure 5-4. Simply click the Close button and the tab closes, removing the Web site from your tab list. Naturally, this closes the tab permanently, so if you are unsure if you want to access the site again in the future, you might consider adding it your Favorites list first.

Figure 5-4

Click the tab, and then click the Close button to close the tab.

Step 3: See All Tabs in One Window

You can easily see your tabs by clicking them, but you can also see a small preview of each tabbed Web site in the same browser window. This feature enables you to take a global look at everything you have tabbed at the moment.

On the toolbar, click the Quick Tabs button (or press CTRL+Q). This action opens all of the Web pages in a single window where you get a mini-view of each Web page, shown in Figure 5-5. Notice that you have a Close button for each Web page, so you can close the tabs you no longer want. You can also click a Web page here to open a full view it. Or you can right-click the page and click Open or Close, or you can close all other tabs in the same way. As you can see, the Quick Tabs option gives you a global look at what you're browsing and makes the management of tabs easy.

Step 4: Saving Tabs

Let's say you've found 10 Web sites that are useful to you, but you need to stop browsing and close Internet Explorer. You can save the tabs for future use, and you can even tell Internet Explorer to reopen the tabs the next time you start the browser.

Figure 5-5

Use Quick Tabs to get a quick view of all tabs.

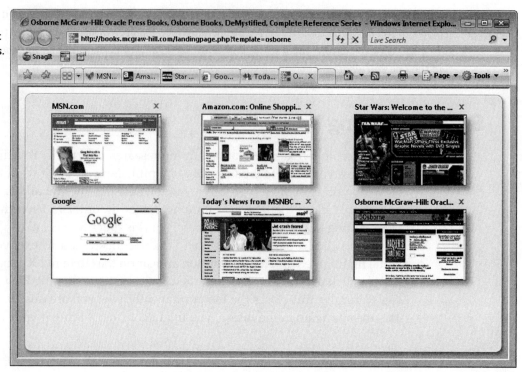

Saving Tabs

To save a collection of tabs that you have made, click the Add To Favorites button on the toolbar (or press ALT+Z). In the drop-down menu that appears, choose Add Tab Group To Favorites. A dialog box appears, shown in the following illustration, where you can give your current tab group a name. Type a name for the group, and click the Add button.

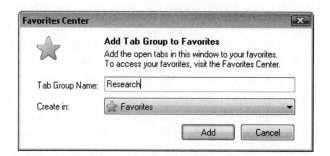

Opening Saved Tabs

Once you save your tab group, you can reopen individual Web pages within the group, or you can open the entire tab group at one time. Open Internet Explorer, and then click the Favorites Center button on the toolbar (or press ALT+C). Click the tab group name, and you will see an expansion list of the tabs in the group. Click the individual Web sites to open them. However, if you want to open the entire group at once, click the arrow that appears to the right of the tab group name, shown in the following illustration. This will open all of the tabs at once.

Make a Group of Tabs Automatically Reopen

Let's say you want to close Internet Explorer, but you want your current group of tabs to automatically reopen the next time you start Internet Explorer. You can easily do this.

Click the Close button to close Internet Explorer. You'll see a dialog box appear asking if you want to close all tabs, as shown in the following illustration. Click the Show Options button on the dialog box, and you'll see a check box to open the tabs the next time you use Internet Explorer. Select this check box and then click Close Tabs. The next time you start Internet Explorer, your group of tabs will automatically open.

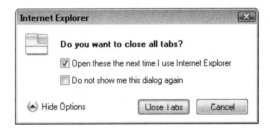

Step 5: Choose Tabbed Browsing Options

Internet Explorer gives you some tabbed browsing options that you can select. You can also choose to stop using tabbed browsing altogether, if you like. These settings are configured in Internet Options.

First, click Tools | Internet Options. On the General tab, you will see a Tabs category, as shown in Figure 5-6. Click the Settings button.

Figure 5-6

Click Settings in the Tabs area to change your tabbed browsing options.

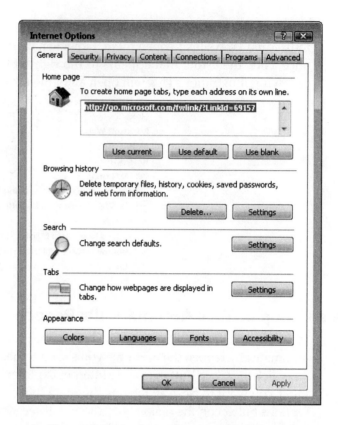

As you can see in Figure 5-7, you have some tabbed browsing options. First, you can disable tabs altogether by clearing the Enable Tabbed Browsing check box. However, if you want to continue using tabbed browsing, you can review the check boxes available to you. The default options are typically all you need, but you can enable or disable these self-explanatory options as desired. Keep in mind that you can always return to the Tabbed Browsing Settings window and make changes at any time.

Figure 5-7

The Tabbed Browsing Settings dialog box

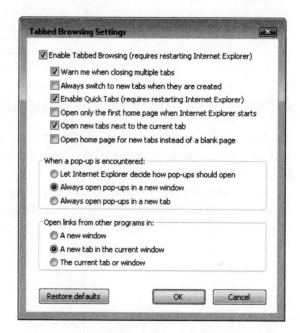

Project 6

Make Work Easier with Windows Meeting Space

What You'll Need:

- Windows Vista: Any version
- Cost: Free

You know the meetings at the board room, city hall, the garden club—wherever. You sit around a table and hash out ideas until you get a consensus. It's the way things typically work. Yet, what do you do if you need to have a meeting with people spread out all over the state, the country, or the world? With Windows Vista and an Internet connection, you can have a virtual meeting using the new Windows Meeting Space feature. With Windows Meeting Space, you can easily share documents, programs, and even your desktop with other people, any time, anywhere. In other words, you can create a virtual meeting room right on your computer and invite up to 10 people to join in. In this project, you'll find out how!

Step 1: Set Up Windows Meeting Space

With Windows Meeting Space, you can collaborate on and share documents and programs, as well as your desktop, with the people invited to the meeting. The other computer users must be using Windows Vista, but their computers can reside on your local network, the Internet, or you can even create an ad hoc wireless network between wireless computers. No matter how the computers are connected, as long as everyone is using Windows Vista, you can use Windows Meeting Space.

In order to begin using Windows Meeting Space, the People Near Me feature must be activated, files must be replicated, and Windows Firewall must be configured for Windows Meeting Space. Fortunately, Windows Vista can do all of these things for you automatically.

Click Start | All Programs | Windows Meeting Space. You'll see a dialog box appear, shown in Figure 6-1, asking if you are ready to set up Windows Meeting Space. Click Yes to continue.

Figure 6-1

Configure Windows
Meeting Space.

As your system is configured for Windows Meeting Space, the People Near Me dialog box is likely to appear, shown in Figure 6-2. Choose your display name, choose if you want the program to start when Windows starts (this is a good idea), and decide if you want to allow invitations from anyone or only from trusted contacts. For the best functionality, keep the "anyone" option enabled. Click OK.

Figure 6-2

People Near Me
dialog box

Once your system is configured, the Windows Meeting Space dialog box appears, shown in Figure 6-3. As it is, the dialog box is not too exciting, but you have to start using it for Windows Meeting Space to be something worthwhile. The following steps will show you how.

Figure 6-3

Windows Meeting
Space

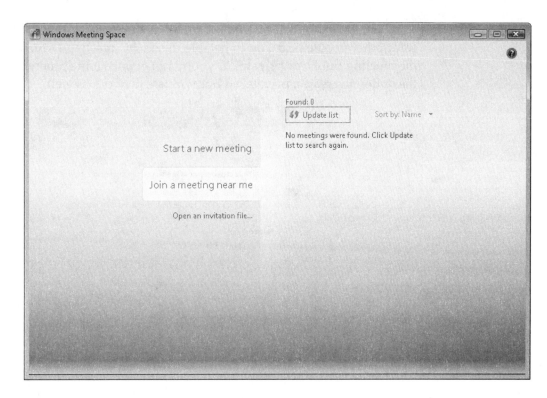

Step 2: Start a New Meeting

Now that you're set up and ready to use Windows Meeting Space, your first task is to start a new meeting. In Windows Meeting Space, click Start A New Meeting. Type a name for the meeting, and enter a password, which must be at least eight characters long, as shown in Figure 6-4.

Figure 6-4

Choose a meeting
name and password.

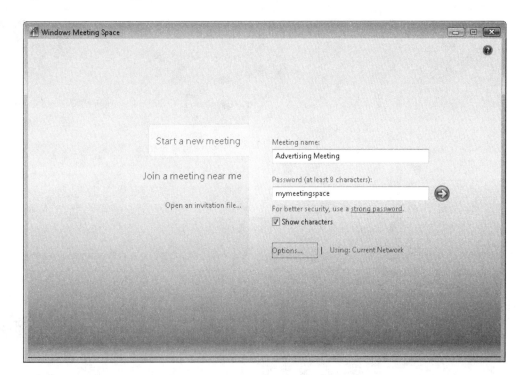

Click the Options link. In the Options dialog box, you can choose whether you want other people near you to be able to see this meeting (which essentially makes the meeting public or private). If you're not connected to a network, you'll also see the option to create a private, ad hoc wireless network as well.

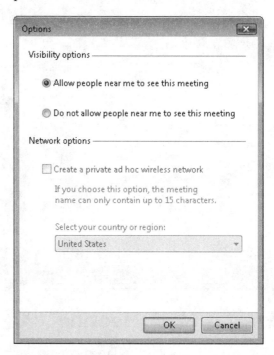

When you're done, click the green arrow button to create the meeting. Once the meeting is created, you'll see the meeting space, shown in Figure 6-5.

Figure 6-5

Meeting space

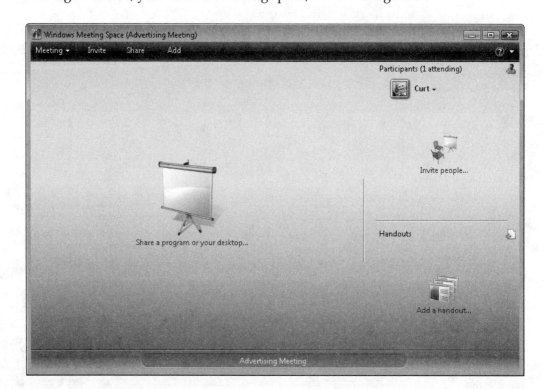

Step 3: Invite People to the Meeting

Once you have your meeting space created, you can invite people to your meeting. In the meeting space, click the Invite People icon. There are three ways that you can invite people:

- If you already have people near you (meaning, they are already connected on your network), they will appear in a dialog box once you click Invite People. Just click the check boxes next to their names, and click the Send Invitations button.

- If you want to invite people who are not near you, you can do so with an e-mail message. Click Invite People in the meeting space, and then click Invite Others. Choose the Send An Invitation In E-Mail option. This will open an e-mail message with the meeting file attached so that others can join the meeting, as shown in the following illustration.

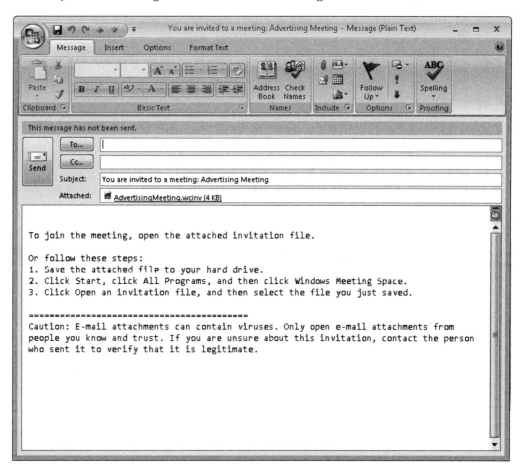

- Finally, you can create an invitation file and get it to meeting recipients in another way. Just click Invite People | Invite Others | Create An Invitation File | Save.

Step 4: Share Items at the Meeting

Now that you have invited people to your meeting, you can share files, programs, and even your desktop if you like. Click the Share A Program Or Your Desktop icon in the meeting space, or click the Share button on the toolbar. Click OK in response to the message about others seeing your desktop. You'll then see a dialog box, shown in Figure 6-6, where you can choose a program, share your desktop, or use the Browse button to browse for a file to open and share.

Figure 6-6

Share items in your meeting.

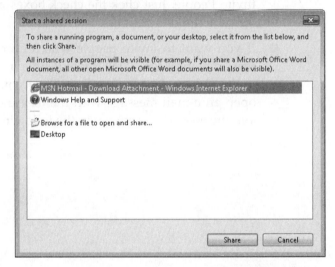

Make your selections. The appropriate programs will be opened, and items you have selected will be shared. As you can see in Figure 6-7, the item you are now sharing appears listed in the meeting space. Notice that you can see how the shared session looks on other computers and you can also stop sharing the item at any time.

Figure 6-7

Shared document in the meeting space

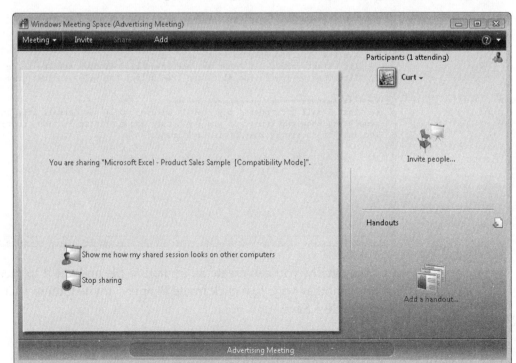

Step 5: Add a Handout to the Meeting

When you add a handout for a meeting, a copy of the file you choose is copied to each meeting participant's computer. This is a quick and easy way to share a file with other users, which they will keep once the meeting has ended.

Figure 6-8

Handouts at this meeting

Click the Handout icon in the meeting space, and then browse for the item you want to share. The handout item will appear in the Handouts section of the meeting space and will be copied to other meeting participants' computers.

Note that participants can make changes to the handout. Those changes are then copied to the other participants' handouts so that everyone always has the same handout. This is a great way to brainstorm together. However, the original handout is not affected by this editing process.

note *During a meeting, you always maintain control of your desktop and programs. You can pass control to someone else temporarily by clicking the Give Control button, but you can always take it back by clicking Take Control or pressing the Windows logo key+ESC.*

View and Manage Photos with Windows Photo Gallery

What You'll Need

- Windows Vista: Any version
- Cost: Free

I'll admit it: I am a photo junkie. No matter what I do, I have my digital camera with me. I take photos of everything my kids do, everywhere we go, every new landscape I see…you name it. The great thing about digital photos is that you buy no film, but the potential bad thing is storing, organizing, and working with photos on your computer. I have folders and folders of photos on my computer, and in previous versions of Windows, I needed software to help me manage and edit those photos.

With Windows Vista, however, Microsoft gives you a new tool called Windows Photo Gallery. The gallery, however, is more than a way to simply look at your photos. You can tag them for easier searching, and you have some basic editing, printing, and storage features. Naturally, this tool is not a replacement for more advanced photo-editing software, but it is a great tool for quick and easy photo management.

Step 1: Open Windows Photo Gallery

The cool thing about Windows Photo Gallery is that it is not obtrusive. You can open a folder of photos on your computer and glance through them, and Windows Photo Gallery doesn't jump to life every time you try to do something with a photo. However, you can also easily open the Photo Gallery and add a folder of photos so that you can work with those photos.

Click Start | All Programs | Windows Photo Gallery. The gallery comes to life, as you can see in Figure 7-1. Click the File menu and choose Add Folder To Gallery. You can then browse for a desired folder of photos or videos that you can add to the

Figure 7-1

Windows Photo
Gallery

gallery for viewing and management purposes. Note that this doesn't change your original folder of photos. That folder stays the same and stays in the same place on your computer. The gallery simply allows you to manage those photos. Notice also that you can use the File menu to import photos directly from a scanner or camera. If you choose this option, you'll see a window where you can choose a device to import the photos from.

Step 2: Use the Control Bar

If you take a look at the bottom of the Windows Photo Gallery, you'll notice a control bar where you can perform some basic actions on your photo. As you can see in the following illustration, the control bar gives you the following controls:

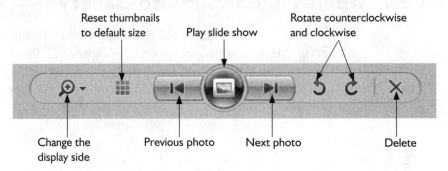

- **Change the display side**   Use this slider bar to quickly change the display size of the photos you see in the gallery.

- **Reset thumbnails to default size**   If you make a change to the display size using the slider bar, you can quickly click this button to return the photos to their default viewing size.

- **Previous photo**   Click this button to move to the previous photo.

- **Play slide show**   Click this button to play a slideshow of your photos.

- **Next photo**   Click this photo to go to the next photo in the gallery.

- **Rotate counterclockwise and clockwise**   Use these two buttons to rotate photos.

- **Delete**   Use this button to move a selected photo to the Recycle Bin.

Step 3: Fix a Photo

If you select a photo and click the Fix button on the toolbar, you'll see an enlarged version of the photo and a control pane that gives you some basic photo-fixing options, as you can see in Figure 7-2.

Figure 7-2

You can choose from several options when fixing a photo.

You have the following options:

- **Auto Adjust**   Click this button, and the gallery will automatically attempt to adjust the color tones in the photo. In some cases, this feature can help to instantly fix a photo; while in others, you may not like the adjustment. If you don't like the adjustment, click the Undo button at the bottom of the control pane.

- **Adjust Exposure**   If you click this button, the control pane gives you two slider bars to adjust the brightness and contrast of the photo, as you can see in the following illustration. You can move these around and see the effect they have on the photo.

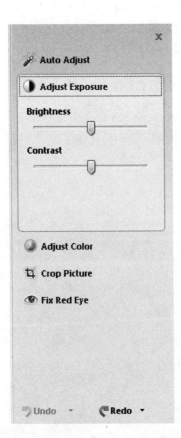

- **Adjust Color**   If you click this button, you'll see slider controls for color temperature, tint, and saturation. Move this around to see the changes that are made on your photo, as you can see in the following illustration.

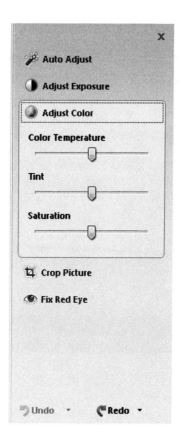

- **Crop** If you click the Crop button, a crop box appears on the photo and a proportion control appears on the pane, shown in Figure 7-3. You can choose the original option so that you can crop in any way that you want, or you can choose a preset, standard print size, such as 4 × 6. This feature enables you to crop the photo but keep a standard print ratio so that the photo will print normally. Make a selection and then drag the crop box around as needed. Then click the Apply button to crop the photo.

- **Fix Red Eye** You can easily remove red eye from a photo. Red eye is a common photo problem that occurs typically in lower light settings. The flash bounces off the blood vessels and tissue of the eye making that wonderful vampire look. You can fix this easily with the gallery. Click the Fix Red Eye button, and then drag your mouse over the red eyes. The gallery will automatically fix the color.

Step 4: Add Info to a Photo

Click the Info button on the toolbar to add a rating to the photo and tags. The rating and tags enable you to add information to the photo so that you can search for it in the future based on this information and find it more easily. For example, you can search for "four star" photos or photos that have certain tags.

Figure 7-3

Crop feature

Once you click the Info button, notice that you can click the stars and assign the photo a general rating. If you are consistent in your use of it, this feature can help you determine what photos in your collection are five-star photos, four-star photos, and so forth.

Next, you can add tags. Tags are labels that are assigned to a photo, enabling you to browse through the tabs in the gallery and see the photos with those tags, or you can search for photos with the tags you're looking for. For example, in Figure 7-4, I have applied the tags "ocean" and "vacation" to the photo. To add a tag, click the Add Tags option, and type the name of the tag.

Also notice that you can add a caption to the photo. Simply click the option, and type the caption that you want to see with the photo.

Step 5: Print Your Photo

You can use the gallery to print your photo. If you click the Print button on the toolbar, you'll have the options to print locally or to order prints on the Internet. If you choose to print your pictures locally, the Print Pictures window will open, shown in Figure 7-5. Here, you can choose the size of your photo, the number of copies, the printer you want to use, and so forth in order to print your photo to your specifications.

Figure 7-4

Add a rating, tags, and caption to a photo.

Figure 7-5

The Print Pictures window

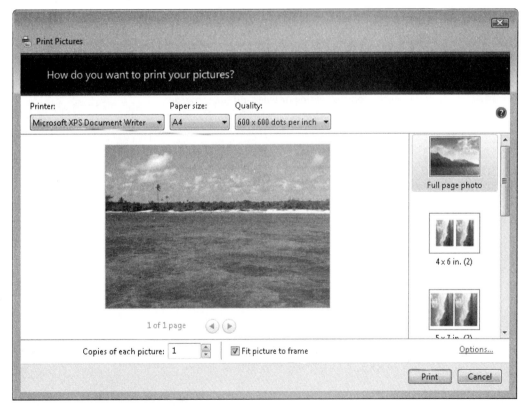

If you choose to order prints online, a dialog box will appear where you can select a printing company to connect to and upload your photos. This process is self-explanatory.

Step 6: E-mail Your Photo

If you click the E-mail button on the toolbar, you'll see a dialog box that enables you to choose the size of your photo and attach it to an e-mail message. Since large photos can be difficult and slow to e-mail to other people, you can adjust the size and see how large in terms of bytes the photo will be for transmission. Typically, an 800 × 600 photo is a good size to consider for sending in e-mail.

Step 7: Burn Your Photos

If you click the Burn button on the toolbar, you can choose whether you want to burn a data disc (CD) or a video DVD. You'll need to insert the CD or DVD and then follow the additional instructions that appear.

Step 8: Make a Movie

Clicking this button on the toolbar opens Windows Movie Maker. The photo or photo collection is transferred to Windows Movie Maker, where you can organize the photos or videos into a movie. You can learn how to make a simple movie using Windows Movie Maker in Project 12.

note   *You'll also see an Open button on the toolbar. Use this button to open the currently selected photo in another photo-editing or video-editing program.*

Use Windows Calendar to Manage Your Life

What You'll Need

- **Windows Vista: Any version**
- **Cost: Free**

I wish I was rich enough to have a personal assistant follow me around all day. From my writing to my teaching deadlines and schedules, it's enough to make my head spin. I'm sure your schedule feels much the same way. After all, we are busy people in the modern world, and we all could use a little help staying organized. The good news is that Windows Vista includes a new tool called Windows Calendar that does just that. In the past, you had to rely on a third-party calendar software package or Microsoft Outlook for a good calendar. Not so in Windows Vista. The calendar is built directly into the operating system so that you can keep track of your appointments and tasks. In fact, you can even publish your calendar on your Web site so that you can look at it even when you're not at home. Best of all—the calendar is easy and quick to use, and in this project, I'll show you how to make the most of it.

Step 1: Explore Windows Calendar

You can open Windows Calendar by clicking Start | All Programs | Windows Calendar. As you can see in Figure 8-1, Windows Calendar provides you with a simple interface that you'll be able to figure out and use in no time. You have the following general areas:

- **Menu bar** The menu bar contains typical Windows menus, such as File, Edit, View, Share, and Help. You can access these menus to use your calendar and configure it.

- **Toolbar** The toolbar contains items that you'll typically use, such as a New Appointment button, New Task button, and so forth.

Figure 8-1

Windows Calendar

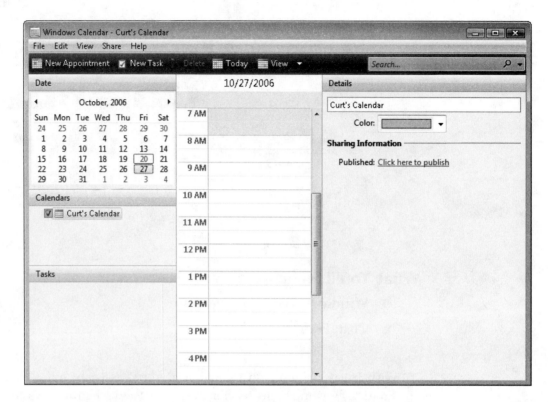

- **Navigation pane**   On the left side of the interface, you see the Navigation pane, which contains the current month's calendar, a list of additional calendars you have created (if any), and a list of any tasks you have made (if any).

- **Day column**   In the day column, you see the current day selected on the calendar to the left. Here, you'll see appointments and tasks for the day. You can switch from day view to work week, week, or month view by clicking the View menu on the toolbar.

- **Details pane**   On the right side of the calendar, you see a details pane for the current calendar, including color options and sharing options.

Step 2: Create Appointments and Tasks

Two primary features of Windows Calendar are appointments and tasks. You can create appointments and tasks, and have the calendar remind you of them as they get close. Both of these procedures are easy and quick. The following two sections show you how to create appointments and tasks.

Create a New Appointment

To create a new appointment, click the New Appointment button on the toolbar. The Details pane now displays the new appointment options. Simply work through the fields on the details pane, and enter the correct information for your appointment. Make sure you choose a start and end time for your appointment and choose a recurrence or reminder option if desired. As you can see in Figure 8-2, I have created an appointment. When you're done, you'll see the appointment appear as a block of time on the day column in the center of the interface, as shown in Figure 8-3.

Figure 8-2

Create a new appointment.

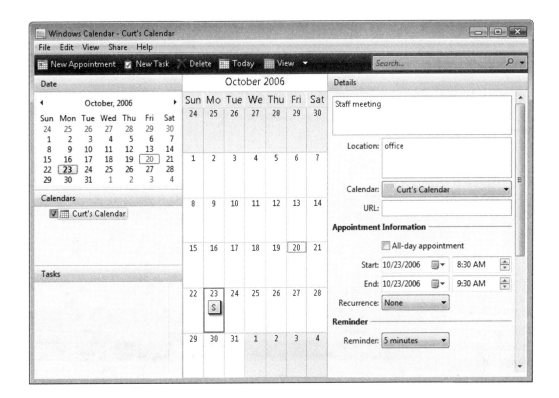

> **tip**   *Need to make a change to an appointment? No problem—just click the appointment, and the detail pane will change back to the appointment. You can then edit it as necessary. You can also delete an appointment by selecting it and clicking the Delete button on the toolbar or by right-clicking the appointment and clicking Delete.*

Create a New Task

Whereas appointments are meetings and events that you need to attend, tasks are simply another kind of appointment to help you remember to get certain things done. You can create a new task by clicking the New Task button on the toolbar. When you do, the Details pane changes to display task information that is similar to the appointment details. Simply fill in the fields and give the task a name, and it will appear in the Tasks section on your calendar. As you can see in Figure 8-4, I have added a task to my day.

Figure 8-3

The new appointment
appears on the calendar.

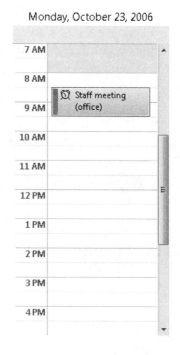

Figure 8-4

Tasks appear in the
Tasks section of the
Navigation pane.

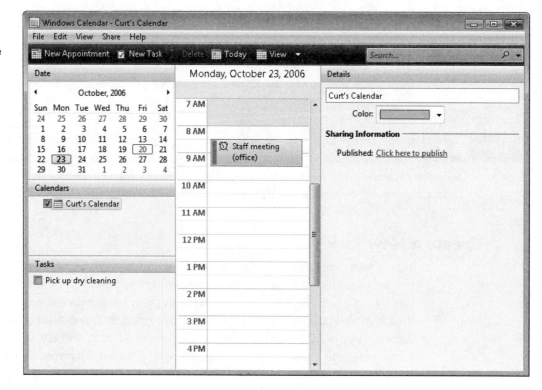

Step 3: Create More Calendars

Windows Calendar will let you create more than one calendar. Let's say you want a calendar for home appointments and tasks and another for business-related appointments or tasks. No matter why you need an additional calendar, you can create multiple calendars and click to manage them as needed. To create a new calendar, click File | New Calendar. The new calendar appears in the Calendars section on the Navigation pane. Type a name for the calendar, and then choose a calendar color in the Details pane. As you can see in Figure 8-5, I now have two calendars. Click the calendar you want to select it, and then add appointments and tasks as necessary.

Figure 8-5

You can create additional calendars.

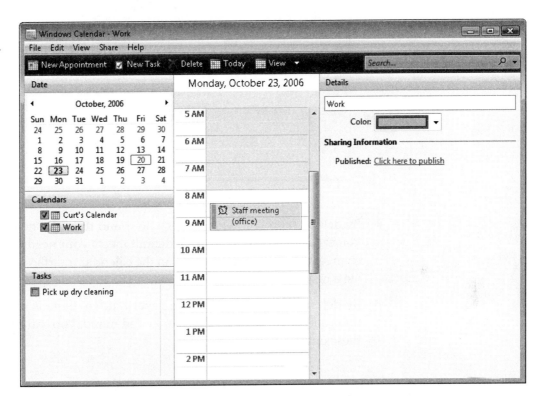

Step 4: Choose Calendar Options

If you click File | Options, you can choose a few default features of your calendar, as shown in Figure 8-6. The following list gives you a few pointers to keep in mind when configuring your calendar:

- By default, the first day of the week is Sunday and the start time for the day is 8:00 a.m. You can change these defaults to whatever you want using the drop-down menus.

- By default, reminders appear in Windows Vista with sound, even if Windows Calendar is not running. This is probably the best setting, because you will not need Windows Calendar open for it to work with your appointments and tasks.

Figure 8-6

Calendar options

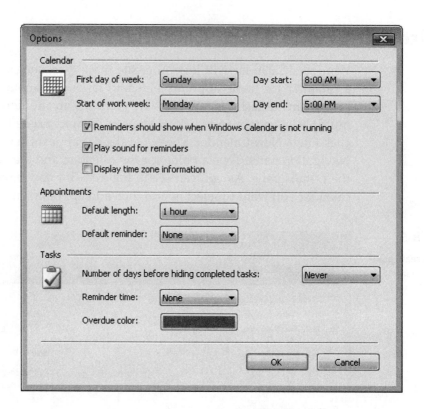

- By default, appointments last one hour and there are no default reminders. You can change this so that the default meets your needs (naturally, you can change it to whatever you want in the calendar interface every time you create a new appointment).

- By default, completed tasks are never hidden, there is no default reminder time, and overdue tasks are color-coded in red. You can change any or all of these options as desired.

Share Your Calendar

Windows Calendar has a feature that makes sharing your calendar or putting it on your Web site easy. If you click the Share option, you'll see that you can publish your calendar, subscribe to an existing Windows Calendar on a Web site, or send your calendar via e-mail. If you click the Publish option, you'll see a single window, shown in Figure 8-7, where you can choose a server location and choose to automatically publish changes to the calendar on the Internet. Naturally, the calendar doesn't provide you with a Web site or permission to access the Web site; this is something you'll need to set up or, in the case of a business Web site, get additional instructions and permissions from the Web site administrator.

Figure 8-7

Options to publish
your calendar

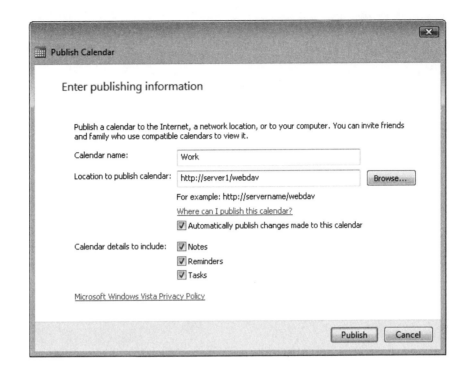

Create a Quick Multimedia Slide Show

What You'll Need

- **Windows Vista: Any version**
- **Cost: Free**

Let's say you have a collection of video and photo files. You attend a meeting at work, and you're asked about a project relating to those video and photo files. You may think, "I wish I had put those together in a Microsoft PowerPoint presentation so that I could show my team." The good news —you don't have to. You can show your team a quick slide show directly from the folder that holds the photos and video files. It's quick, easy, and something you can use for your own personal enjoyment or at the office, depending on your needs.

The slide show uses Windows Photo Gallery, which you can learn more about in Project 7. In this project, we'll focus specifically on using the slide show feature.

Step 1: Get Your Files Together

The slide show feature works on a folder basis, so your first task when using the slide show is to first get all of the photos or video files you want to see in the slide show into the same folder. Keep in mind that the slide show feature only plays photo or video files. You can have other documents or files in the folder, but the slide show will ignore them. For example, let's say you have a work project with video files, photos, and several Microsoft Excel documents. You can store all of these items in the same folder, but quickly jump to a slide show when necessary, and the slide show will ignore the Excel documents since they are not slide show material.

As you gather your files into a folder, keep in mind that the slide show will rotate through them in the order in which they are organized in the folder. Therefore, you may want to drag the icons around within the folder to order them in a way that makes sense for your slide show. As you can see in Figure 9-1, I have a folder that contains a movie and four photos. In the current order, the movie will play first and then the photos will follow in order. I can drag these around within the folder to change the order.

Figure 9-1

Organize your photo
and video files.

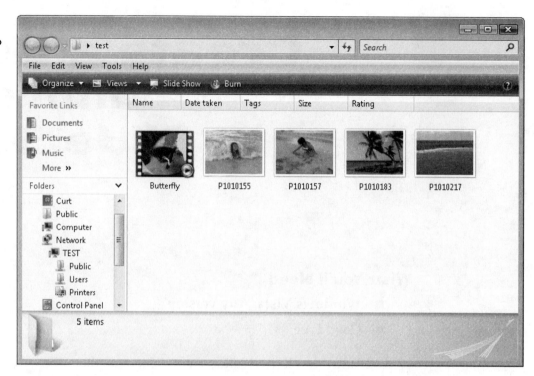

> tip If you're working with a number of photos and video files within a folder, remember to use the
> Views menu to adjust the icon size. This will make organizing and reordering your video and
> photo files easier.

Step 2: Start the Slide Show

You can start the slide show at any time by opening your folder of video and photo files and clicking the Slide Show button on the toolbar. The slide show begins as a full-screen slide show that also contains a control toolbar. The control toolbar will disappear after a moment, but all you have to do is move your mouse over the area toward the bottom and it will reappear. You can exit the slide show by clicking Exit on the toolbar or pressing ESC on your keyboard.

The slide show toolbar provides basic play, forward, and back controls, but you also have an Options menu. Here, you can choose the speed of the slide show's automatic rotation, shuffle the photos and video, loop them so that they play over and over until you stop it, and mute the sound.

On the Themes menu, you can choose among different themes that give your slide show different looks, depending on your needs. Review these options and see which ones you like best. If you're showing a slide show of photos, consider using the Pan And Zoom option—it will give your slide show photos a sense of slight movement, which creates more visual interest.

note *If you don't see any slide show controls, your slide show is running in Basic mode. Basic mode is used if your computer doesn't score at least a 3 in the graphics category of the Windows Experience Index (see what your score is by accessing the Welcome Center). In Basic mode, you can't control the theme or other aspects of the slide show, but you can right-click the slide show and use certain controls. Also, if you find Basic mode cumbersome, you can play your slide show using Windows Media Player, which is described in the next section. The only way to leave Basic mode is to upgrade your computer's graphics card and possibly your computer's random access memory (RAM) so that the Windows Experience Index is raised to at least a 3.*

Step 3: Use Windows Media Player as a Slide Show

The slide show available through Windows Photo Gallery is quick and easy to use, but if you have problems using it, or if you would rather work through Windows Media Player, you can show your folder of videos and photos there as well.

You open Windows Media Player by clicking Start | All Programs | Windows Media Player. If you click in the Now Playing area, you see a List pane on the right side of the window. If you don't see it, click the Now Playing menu and click Show List Pane. Now, simply drag your folder of photos and videos to the List pane and then click the Play button on the toolbar. Your photos and videos will now begin to play in Windows Media Player, shown in Figure 9-2.

To avoid seeing the List pane during the slide show, click the arrow control on the List pane to close it. You can always turn it back on by clicking Now Playing | Show List Pane. Figure 9-3 shows you the same slide show without the List pane.

Figure 9-2

Slide show in Windows Media Player

Figure 9-3

Slide show without
the List pane

You can also see your slide show as a full-screen slide show with controls. Click the View Full Screen button in the lower-right corner of Windows Media Player to switch to full-screen mode. As you can see in Figure 9-4, the toolbar appears at the bottom of the full-screen mode so that you can still control the slide show.

Figure 9-4

Full-screen mode

Manage the Web Sites Your Children Can View and the Games They Can Play

What You'll Need

- **Windows Vista: Any version**
- **An Internet connection**
- **Cost: Free**

My first computer was a Commodore 64. Yes, I know that dates me a bit. I earned enough money at a summer job to buy that used Commodore 64 computer when I was in the eighth grade, and I thought I was a real computer geek. In those days, my parents didn't have to worry about what games I might play on the computer, what I might do with the computer, or what I might see—there were no "real" computer games, and no one even had a concept of the mammoth public network we now call the Internet.

Things have changed—a lot. My five-year-old daughter knows how to access different Web sites and play games that I have given her access to. My 10-year-old probably knows more about the computer and Internet surfing than I would like to admit, and as a parent, that worries me. I know all too well what dangers are just a click away, and as a parent, I am pleased to tell you that Windows Vista's parental controls are great. They work well, and are quick and easy to configure and use. Let me say it bluntly: *If you have children who use the computer, you must use parental controls.* This project shows you how!

 See a CNET video on keeping your kids safe online at http://diyvista.cnet.com

Step 1: Create a User Account for Your Children

Parental controls are specific computer settings that are applied to a user account. As such, you should have a password-protected user account on your computer that runs Windows Vista, but your child should have his or her own account. This way, you can apply the parental controls to your child's account without placing restrictions on your account. You can create a user account for your children quickly and easily.

Open User Accounts

Click Start | Control Panel. In Control Panel, click the Add Or Remove User Accounts link under the User Accounts And Family Safety section, as shown in Figure 10-1.

Figure 10-1

Click Add Or Remove User Accounts to get started.

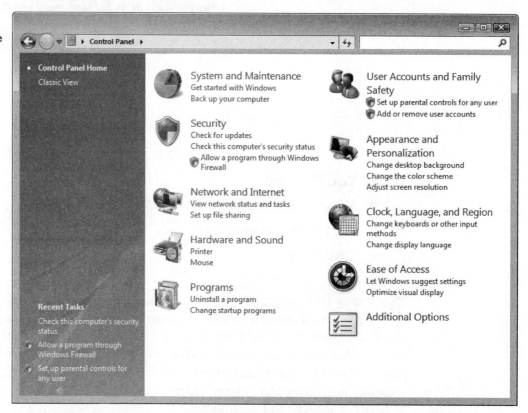

The User Accounts interface opens, as you can see in Figure 10-2. You'll see the account you created when you installed Windows Vista and a Guest account, which is probably turned off. Notice the Create A New Account link. Click this link to create the new account for your child.

Create the New User Account

In the window that opens, you can create the new user account for your child, shown in Figure 10-3. First, give the account a name. Since your child will be logging on to

Figure 10-2

Choose to create a new account.

Figure 10-3

Create the new user account for your child.

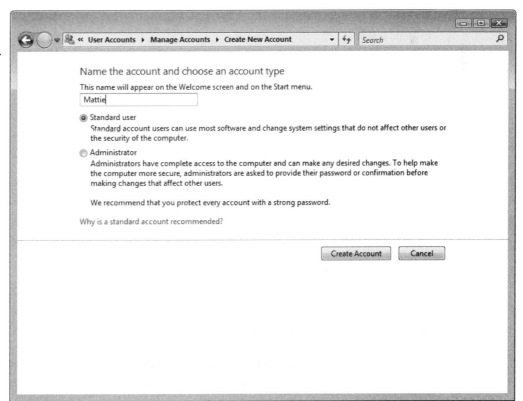

the computer using this account, it's easiest to give the account your child's name (or a nickname, if you prefer). By default, the Standard user option is selected. This setting is a restricted setting that allows the user to access software and even change system settings that do not affect the security of the computer. On the other hand, you have an Administrator option, which essentially gives the user the ability to change settings that affect every user and the computer's security. You should never give your child administrator privileges, so keep the Standard user option selected. Click the Create Account button.

You now see the new account appear in the User Accounts window (see Figure 10-2). Click your child's new account. You now see the option to make changes to the user account, such as creating a password, changing the picture, and such, shown in Figure 10-4. Because my children are young, I don't create passwords for them. All they have to do when they start Windows is click their user names. Older children may want passwords to ensure some sense of privacy.

Figure 10-4

You can customize your child's account.

You can click the *Change The Picture* link and choose a photo that your child likes. You can also click the *Browse For More Pictures* link and choose a photo of your own. Consider using the Browse option and using a photo of your child's face. Younger children love this feature because they see their name and photo at the Windows logon screen!

Step 2: Setting Up Parental Controls

Now that you have your child's user account created, you can set up parental controls for that child. Click Start | Control Panel. Under the User Accounts And Family

Safety area, click Set Up Parental Controls For Any User. In the window that opens, click your child's user account to set up the controls. This opens the parental controls window for that user, shown in Figure 10-5.

 Your administrator account must use a password. If you don't have one, your children can simply open your account and change the parental controls you configure. In addition, the password should be one that your children cannot guess, preferably one that uses random letters and numbers.

To begin the process, first turn on parental controls by selecting the On option. You can now configure some settings that will control what your child can and can't do, as you can see in the Windows Settings area of the screen (see Figure 10-5).

Figure 10-5

Parental controls for
the selected user

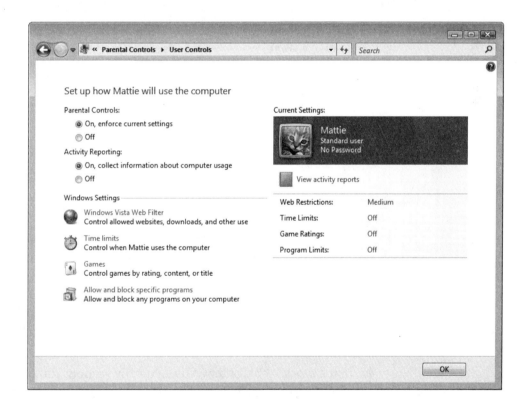

Configure the Windows Vista Web Filter

The first control area you can configure is the Windows Vista Web filter. This control enables you to place restrictions on Internet usage. Click the Windows Vista Web Filter link to open the Web Filter window, shown in Figure 10-6.

When configuring the Web filter:

- The first two options allow you to block some Web content or not. If you choose the "allow" option, the Internet is an open book for your child. It's best to keep the default setting to block some Web sites and content.

- In the next area, you can choose to allow or block specific Web sites or allow only the Web sites that are on the allow list. I use this feature for my five-year-old. As you can see in the following illustrations, there are only a few sites that I allow her to visit. I have chosen to edit the allow and block lists, entered the sites, and then clicked the Only Allow Websites Which Are On The Allow List check box. Now, the Internet is completely locked down to only these sites, thereby preventing her from stumbling her way on to another Web page. Depending on your child's age, you may want to take this highly controlled approach.

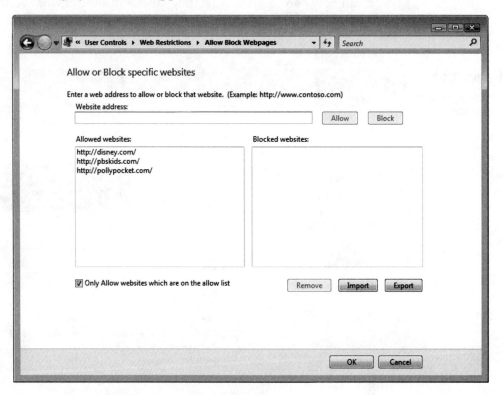

- In the Block Web Content Automatically section, you can choose a restriction level for your child. The High or Medium option is typically best, depending on your child's age. You can click each option here and read a summary of what is blocked. You might also want to click the How Does The Web Filter Work? link to read a summary. Note that if you choose to allow only Web sites that are on the allow list, this entire section is unavailable to you because site access is completely controlled by the allow list.

 The Web filter significantly reduces the likelihood of your child accessing objectionable material on the Internet, but it is not foolproof. What is "objectionable" is highly subjective, so even with a setting configured here, you should still personally monitor what your child is accessing. Parental controls also enable you to monitor what your child has been doing with the computer. You'll see how later in this project.

Figure 10-6

Windows Vista
Web filter

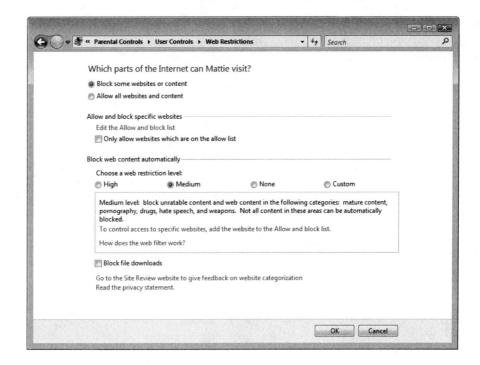

● The last setting you can enable is to block file downloads. Selecting this check box stops the ability to download any files from the Internet. For younger children, this is a good setting to enable because it prevents the possible downloading of information you may not want to them to have.

Control Time Limits

The next setting you can configure in the parental controls window is time limits. If you click the Time Limits link, you will see a calendar where you can control when your child is allowed to use the computer, shown in Figure 10-7. You can use this feature to keep your child from using the Internet during times when you are not home to supervise, or in the middle of the night for an older child or teen. Drag to select the hours and days you want to block, and they will turn blue, indicating they are blocked. White areas mean the time and day are available. If you make a mistake or decide to change the time limits later, click the blue areas to turn them white again.

Control Games Your Child Can Play

If you click the Games link on the parental controls window, you will see a window, shown in Figure 10-8, that allows or disallows game playing, with controls to set game ratings and allow or block specific games on your computer.

If you enable game playing, you can click the Set Game Ratings link and choose to block all games that do not have a rating (this is recommended), and then choose the level of game rating that is allowed, such as early childhood, everyone, everyone 10+, teen, and so forth. Read the summary of the rating level, determine which setting is

Figure 10-7

Click to block the
desired time and days.

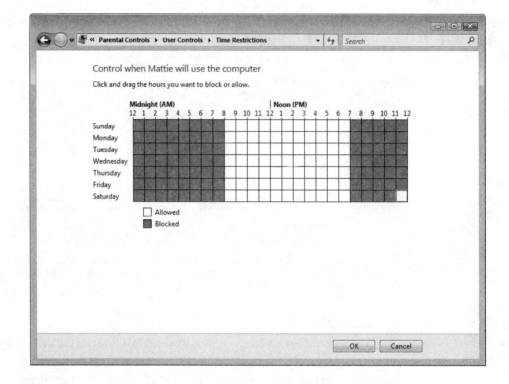

best for your child, and then choose the appropriate option, as shown in the following
illustration. If you scroll through the list, you can select check boxes that block certain

Figure 10-8

Allow or block
game playing.

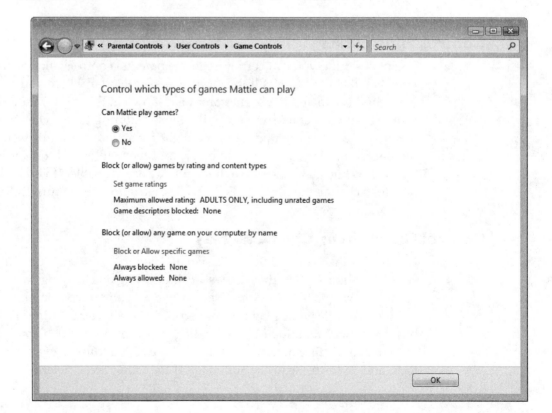

kinds of content, even if the game has an allowed rating. For example, you can block the ability to play the game online, block blood and gore, crude humor, and such. Simply select the relevant check box to enable the desired controls.

You can also choose the option to allow or block specific games on the primary games window. Clicking the Block Or Allow Specific Games link opens another window where you can see the games installed on your computer. Here, you can choose to use the user rating (this option is selected by default for all installed games), or you can choose to always allow or always block certain games. Make your selections and click OK.

Allow or Block Specific Programs

The final setting you can enable in parental controls is to allow or block specific programs installed on your computer. Maybe you have programs installed that you do not want your children to use for various reasons. Click the Allow Or Block Specific Programs link in the parental controls window, and then choose the option that allows your child to only access the programs you have selected. Click OK.

You'll then see a listing of all programs installed on your computer. You need to click the check boxes of the programs that you want your child to be able to use.

All programs not selected are automatically blocked, as you can see in the following illustration. Make your selections and click OK.

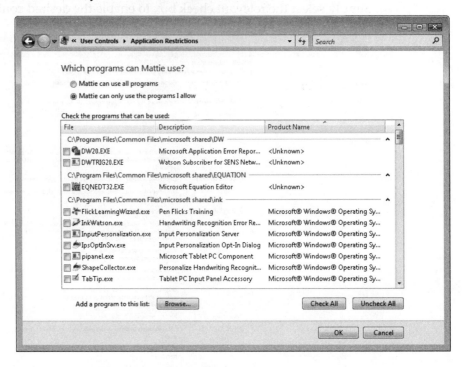

Step 3: View Your Child's Activity Report

If you open the parental controls window for your child's user account, you will see an option to view your child's activity report. This feature is helpful because you can review on a periodic basis what your child is doing on the computer, rather than having to constantly look over your child's shoulder. You can see what your child has done on the Internet, any system changes that have been made, what applications were used, what games were played, any e-mail that has been received or sent, changes to contact information, instant messaging activities, and any media that was viewed. Click the View Activity Reports link, and then use the categories on the left side of the window, shown in Figure 10-9, to see your child's activity.

note *Your child should use Windows Mail for e-mail usage or another program that supports parental controls, such as Microsoft Outlook. Use of Web-based mail or other third-party e-mail applications may not report to parental controls.*

Figure 10-9

Review your child's activities on the computer.

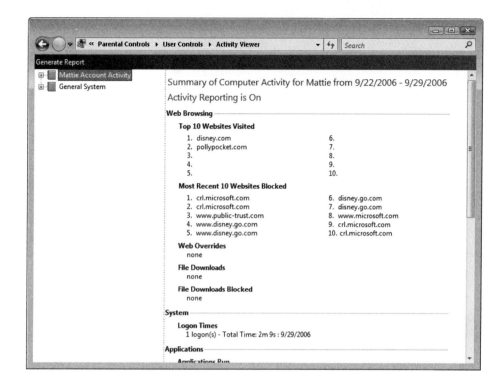

Part II
Challenging

Project 11

Create a Custom CD Cover

What You'll Need

- Windows Vista: Any version
- Digital photos
- CD covers: $10 or less
- Software: At least $40

I make a lot of custom CDs—often several different music CDs a week, each one containing its own compilation of songs. I also put photos on CDs and send them to my mom, friends, and other family members. It's a great way to stay in touch and let them see what the kids have been up to. No matter how you use CDs, you likely know that you can write directly on the front of the disc with a permanent marker and label them. However, you might want something that looks a bit nicer, and that's where this project comes in. You can use Windows Vista to create custom CD covers and print them on adhesive CD labels. The end result is custom covers that look great and really communicate what is on the CD.

Step 1: Gather the Labels and Software

Windows Vista doesn't give you any software that will create CD labels, nor does it give you the labels. You'll need to acquire these two items. However, don't let this be a deterrent, because you'll be able to find CD labels at just about any department or discount store. You can find software for creating the labels on the Internet, and you can even download trial versions of this software and try it out before you buy it. If you choose to buy it, most of the software is inexpensive.

If you used Windows XP in the past (which you probably did), you may remember that Windows XP also had some Plus! Packs that were released, containing different software tools, including a CD-labeling tool. At the time of this writing, Windows Vista doesn't have a Plus! Pack, but it could in the future. So before you buy any software, you might want to check out www.microsoft.com/windowsvista and make sure there is no downloadable software on the Microsoft site.

First things first, you'll need to purchase some CD covers. These are made from photo printing paper with adhesive backs. You run the cover through your printer, and then peel it away from the backing before putting it on your CD. You can purchase different brands and different-sized packs at most discount and department stores, so check them out and choose one for your labels. Memorex makes a good label product, and I've been pleased with the results.

Next, you'll need to choose some software. If you search for CD-labeling software on any search engine, you'll find several different products to choose from. I've downloaded and experimented with several of them. The following sections explain a few of your options and where to get them.

AudioLabel

The AudioLabel software, shown in Figure 11-1, is a nice piece of software that gives you quite a bit of flexibility. It contains a bank of 70 images that you can use as backgrounds (many of them quite entertaining), with a quick text editor, so you can use whatever text you want. You can download and try the AudioLabel software for 15 days, after which you'll have to purchase it for just under $30. I'll use AudioLabel as the example software in the rest of the project. Find out more at www.audiolabel.com.

Figure 11-1

AudioLabel

Label Xpress

Label Xpress is designed to be quick and easy labeling software. Shown in Figure 11-2, I found the interface easy to work with. and you will likely master the product in no time. Thumbnails and clickable tabs make maneuvering easy. However, I found the text-editing portion of the software cumbersome and a bit confusing. You can try the software for free, or you can buy it for just under $10, which makes the product very appealing, considering what you get for your money. Find out more at www.cdlabel4sale.com.

Figure 11-2

Label Xpress

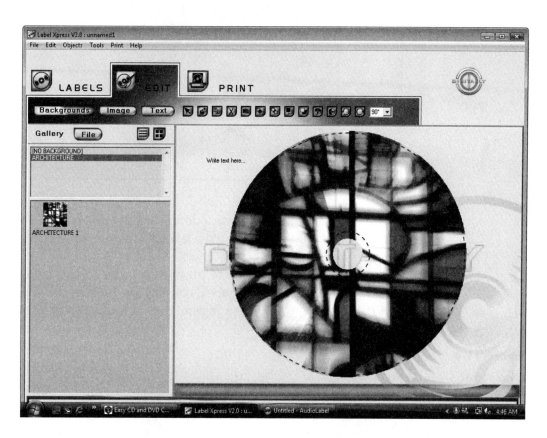

Easy CD & DVD Cover Creator

Here's another CD-labeling software for less than $10. I found this product to be great because the interface is so easy to use. You just click a few buttons, put what you want on the CD, and you're done! The flip side is that you don't have as much flexibility as you do with other products (see Figure 11-3). However, if you know that you'll create a lot of labels that are similar in nature, this may be a good product for you because it is so quick and easy. Download a trial version and find out more www.easycoverdesign.com.

Step 2: Choose the Layout

Now that you have selected your label paper and software, you can get started creating your own label. In the rest of this project, I'm going to use AudioLabel for my software (see Step 1). If you want to download this software and try it, you can follow

Figure 11-3

Easy CD & DVD
Cover Creator

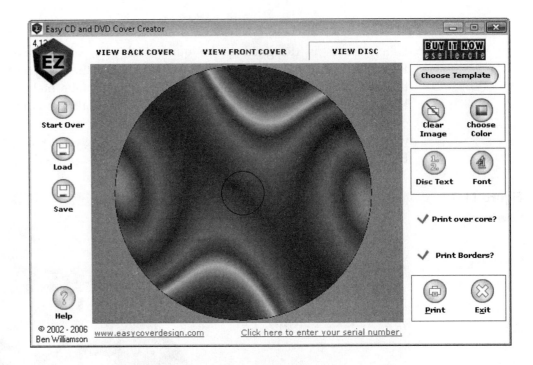

along with me. If you want to use a different software package, simply use the rest of
this project as a guide to creating the label, but not as step-by-step instructions, since
your software is different.

The first thing you'll need to do is choose the correct layout that matches the
labels you bought. In AudioLabel, you can do this by clicking Layout | Change
Label Paper. As you can see in Figure 11-4, you can choose the brand of label that

Figure 11-4

Choose your
label paper.

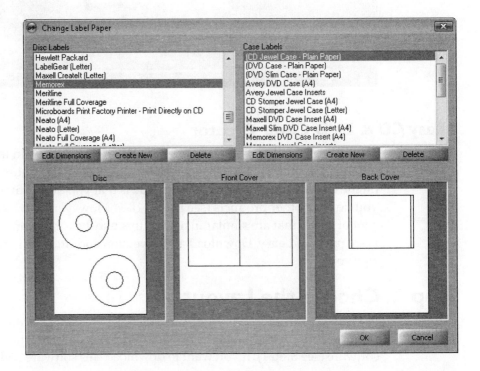

you bought. Select your brand in the list, and click OK. The software will use the item you selected as a template to make sure your label prints correctly on the paper. If you don't see your brand of label listed, scroll through the list, and choose a label that looks most similar to yours.

Step 3: Choose a Color or Background Image

Your next step is to choose a color or background image for the CD cover. Think carefully during this step, because you want something that both looks good and enables you to see your printed text easily. Most programs have background image options, as well as color selection palette if you want to use a plain color.

If I want to use a plain color in AudioLabel, I simply select the color from the color chart at the top of the screen, and the color changes immediately. The text editor appears automatically as well, so I can see how well the color looks under the text.

If you want to use an image, there is an image bank to the right of the screen. Scroll through it, find the image you like, and double-click it to apply it to your cover. As with a simple color, I can see the text on top of the image so that I can know how the text will look with the background, shown in Figure 11-5.

Figure 11-5

Image background

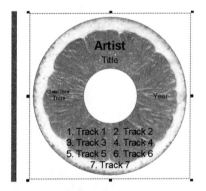

You can also use your own photos as background images. When you do, you'll need to experiment with them to see how the software crops the image and what content you lose because of the hole in the CD. I have even gone to the trouble to crop and resize images in Adobe Photoshop so that the software didn't cut off a person's head I wanted on the cover. Naturally, this is a lot of work, but it is an option. To use your own image, click Image Search and browse for the image you want to use. Once you have the desired image in place, you're ready to move on to text editing.

Step 4: Edit Your Text

With your background in place, you're now ready to add your text. AudioLabel provides default text with an artist name, title, time, year, and track names. You can put all of this on the label, or you can simply remove what you don't want using the text editor. The good news is that the placement of the text is already done for you, so all you have to do is retype the text in the editor and remove anything that you don't want.

As you can see in the following illustration, just retype the desired fields with the text you want. You can leave the ones you don't want blank, and you can immediately see your entries on the label. Use the text editor to make any changes that you want.

Once you've typed text on the label, you can click the text to select it, and then you can change the color of the text, font, size, make it bold, and so on, as shown in Figure 11-6. As you can see, the interface is rather intuitive and easy to work with.

Step 5: Print Your Label

Now you're ready to print your label! Just insert the label sheet into your printer, and click the Print button in AudioLabel. You'll see a simple Print dialog box, shown in Figure 11-7. Here, you can see how your label will be placed on the sheet. Notice that if your sheet has more than one label (many brands have two), you can use the Disc Position drop-down menu to choose which label you want to print to. When you're done, just click the Print button and your label will be sent to the printer.

Figure 11-6

Click the text to change color, font, and other characteristics.

> **tip**   *Since labels that use a background tend to use a lot of ink, you should let the label dry for a few minutes before removing it from the backing and pressing it onto your CD.*

Figure 11-7

Print dialog box

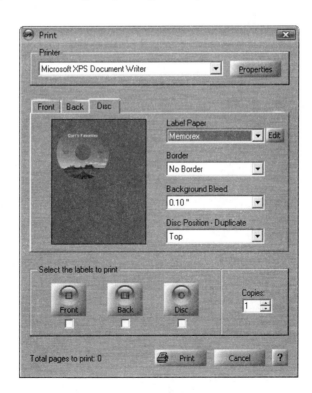

Create a Simple Movie with Digital Video and Photos

What You'll Need

- Windows Vista: Any version
- Video clips and/or photos
- Cost: Free

W indows Vista includes a video-editing program called Windows Movie Maker. It's not new to Windows, but it is certainly improved in this version. When you couple this program with the new Windows DVD Maker, you can quickly create a movie and burn it to a DVD in no time. It's important to note here that Windows Movie Maker is not an advanced video-editing program. The editing and creation abilities you have in Windows Movie Maker are limited, but for a basic program, it works great. Let me also say that this project is not meant to be a treatise about Windows Movie Maker. I want to show you in a few quick steps how to create a basic movie. You can then build on that foundation and add more movie-editing skills using other books if you like. This project is designed to help you create a quick project so that you can see what Windows Movie Maker has to offer. Let's get started!

Step 1: Get Familiar with the Windows Movie Maker Interface

You can open Windows Movie Maker by clicking Start | All Programs | Windows Movie Maker. The Windows Movie Maker interface, see Figure 12-1, provides you with a few important, distinct work areas:

- **Menu** Windows Movie Maker contains a standard menu of options, including File, Edit, View, Tools, Clip, Play, and Help. You'll use these menus to access Windows Movie Maker features as you create movies.

Figure 12-1

Windows Movie
Maker

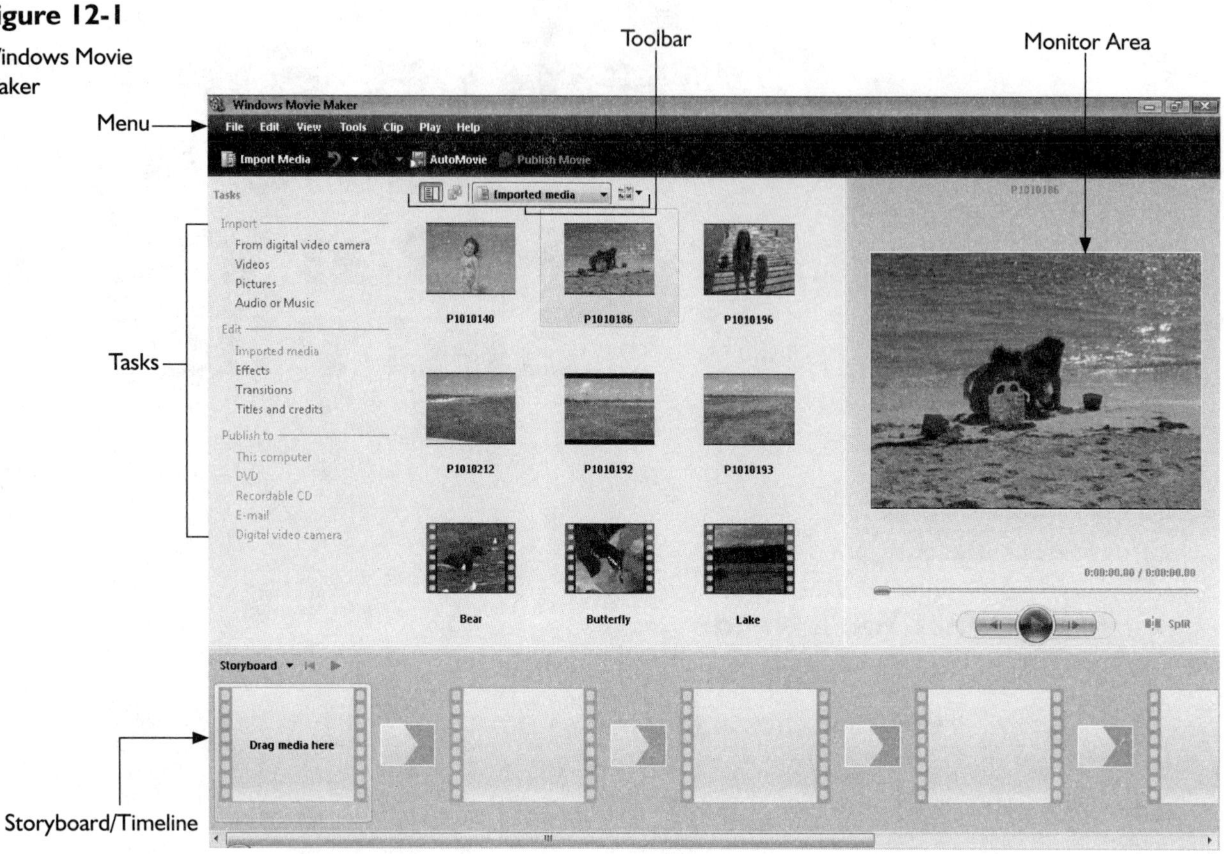

- **Toolbar**   The toolbar provides quick and easy access to common features. The toolbar options you see change, depending on your current task.

- **Tasks**   The Tasks pane, located on the left side of the interface, is your quick and easy access point for all kinds of functions and features. The content of the Tasks pane changes, depending on what you are working on at the moment.

- **Monitor area**   The Monitor area enables you to watch your movie in progress and also manage your clips.

- **Storyboard/Timeline**   The Storyboard and Timeline views enable you to assemble your movie and work with various pieces of it.

Step 2: Import Your Data

You can import digital video and photos directly from your video camera or from your computer, if the files already reside there. You can also import music to use in your movie in the same way.

In terms of connecting your video camera to your computer, you'll need to determine what kind of connection is required. Typically, most video cameras today can connect using a FireWire cable (IEEE 1394) or a Universal Serial Bus (USB) port. Check your camera documentation for more information.

Importing from a Digital Video Camera

You can import directly from your digital video camera. Simply connect your camera to your computer and turn it on. Then:

1. In the Tasks pane, click Import From Digital Video Camera, and then click the Import button.

2. In the Name box, type a name for the video file.

3. Choose a location to save your video file from the Import To list, or click Browse and choose another location.

4. In the Format list, choose either the Windows Media Video (WMV) file format or the AVI format.

5. Click either Import Entire Videotape To My Computer or Only Import Parts Of The Videotape To My Computer, and click Next.

6. Start importing according to the directions on your screen.

Importing Existing Video or Pictures on Your Computer

If you already have video files and/or picture files on your computer, you can import them directly into Windows Movie Maker.

1. In the Tasks pane, under Import, click the Videos option.

2. In the Import Media Items dialog box, shown in the following illustration, browse to locate the desired video files. Select them and click Import.

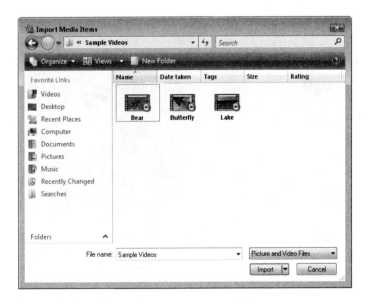

3. Repeat this process, but this time, in the Tasks pane, choose Pictures.

Once you have your items imported, they appear in the Imported Media area (see Figure 12-1).

Step 3: Editing Video

Now that you know how to import data, it's time to turn your attention to editing your video clips. Keep in mind that you can combine video and still shots into one movie and blend them together as desired. Typically, you'll want to cut some segments of video that are boring or that do not add anything to your video. You'll later assemble these clips in the desired order on the storyboard.

Splitting Clips

Windows Movie Maker creates clips for you; however, you may need to split those clips into more manageable pieces. You can perform this function by using the Split command.

1. Select the clip that you want to split in the Collections area.

2. In the Monitor area, click the Play button.

3. When the clip reaches the point at which you want to split it, click the Split Clip button in the Monitor area, as shown in Figure 12-2. You can also click Clip | Split or press CTRL+M on your keyboard. In the Imported Media area, the clip is split in two—the first part of the clip retains its original name, while the second clip contains the original name followed by 1. You can change the name as desired.

Figure 12-2

Click the Split Clip button to split the clip.

0:00:03.57 / 0:00:10.18

Split

Combining Clips

Just as you can split a clip into two or more clips, you can also combine clips as needed. To combine two or more clips:

1. In the Imported Media area, select the clips that you want to combine: select the first clip, hold down the SHIFT key on your keyboard, and select the remaining clips that you want to combine.

2. Choose Clip | Combine. The clips are combined, using the first clip's name for the new file.

Step 4: Assemble Your Movie

You can use the workspace to create a storyboard or to sequence your clips together. You'll drag clips on to the workspace area to create the storyboard. Begin by dragging the first clip in your movie to the video area of the workspace. Once in position, you see the first frame of the video displayed in the Monitor area. If you change to Timeline view, you can see how much time is consumed by the clip. By using the timeline, you can connect pieces of clips while monitoring the time frame of the whole movie. However, you will probably find that Storyboard view, shown in Figure 12-3, is initially easier to use when you are assembling your movie.

Figure 12-3

Storyboard view

If you switch to Timeline view, you can see more information about your movie's time. The zoom in and zoom out buttons at the top of the workspace let you see more detail concerning the timeline (click the Storyboard drop-down menu, and choose Timeline). While zoomed out, the storyboard is shown to you in increments of 10 seconds. You can zoom in and zoom out more to see the clips in whatever time measure you want. Figure 12-4 shows you the Timeline view.

Figure 12-4

Timeline view

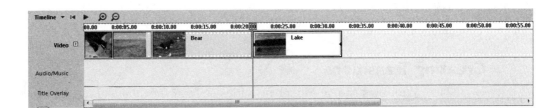

Feel free to mix video and still shots together on the storyboard. By default, imported still shots are given five seconds of time on a storyboard. You can change that value on the timeline by grabbing the edge of a photo and dragging to increase its duration.

Trimming Clips

As you are working with clips in the storyboard, you will notice areas of your video that you want to cut out, or trim. These are often dull spots in the video where not much is happening. For example, let's say you have been videotaping your dog. Your dog does this great trick, but to capture the trick, you end up filming a boring minute or two waiting for the dog to perform. Now you want to lose the boring time when you create the movie—no problem; just trim off the excess.

In reality, the trim feature is powerful because it gives you a fine level of control over your clips. You can use the timeline feature in the Workspace and trim away seconds of a clip that you do not want to use.

1. In the Timeline view, select the clip you want to trim. The first frame of the clip appears in the Monitor area.

2. The trimming process keeps the portion of videotape that you trim and discards the rest. That might seem a little confusing, but think of it as trimming a piece of paper: You trim away the pieces you don't want in order to keep the primary piece.

3. Choose Clip | Trim Beginning or Trim End.

4. In the Timeline view, drag the control handle to trim away a portion of the beginning or end. You may first need to use the magnifier tool to zoom in so that you can see the clip in more detail, as shown in the following illustration.

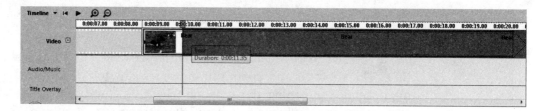

5. If you don't want to keep the trim points you just set, choose Clip | Clear Trim Points.

 As you can probably guess, the trim feature is useful—but a little confusing at first. Spend a few moments playing with the feature until you get the hang of how it works.

Creating Transitions

Windows Movie Maker provides several *transitions* that you can use between clips. You place transitions between clips so that the flow from one to another is more natural and less choppy. This is true of video, photos, or both.

You can easily create transitions in the storyboard.

1. In the workspace, make certain that you are in Storyboard view.

2. In the Tasks pane, under Edit, click Transitions. You can see the available transitions in the content area of the interface, shown in the following illustration.

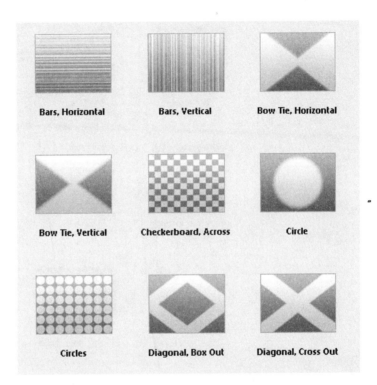

Bars, Horizontal	Bars, Vertical	Bow Tie, Horizontal
Bow Tie, Vertical	Checkerboard, Across	Circle
Circles	Diagonal, Box Out	Diagonal, Cross Out

3. A transition box appears between each clip/photo on the storyboard. Drag a desired transition to a transition box on the storyboard. Each time you place a transition, an icon will appear in the transition box between each clip, as shown in the following illustration.

4. Click Play in the Monitor area to see your movie play with the transitions.

Add Effects

Windows Movie Maker also includes a number of effects you can add to any clip or photo. Effects cover all kinds of video/photo effects, such as blurring features, lighting features, and even an old-age film effect. These features are not necessary, of course, but they can add interest to your movies. To add an effect:

1. In the Tasks pane, under Edit, choose Effects. You'll see the effects options in the collections area, as shown in the following illustration.

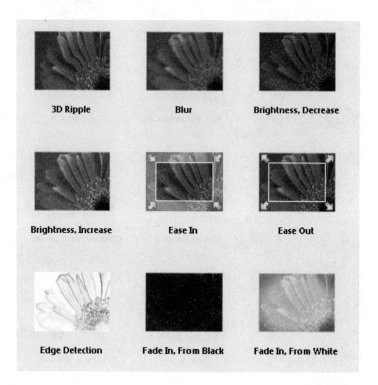

2. Scroll through the effects, and locate one that you want to use.

3. Drag the effect to the star icon on the desired clip in the storyboard, as shown in the following illustration. Repeat this process for other clips to which you want to add effects.

4. Click Play in the Monitor area to see your effect in action.

tip *If you add an effect that you don't like, just click Edit | Undo or right-click the star area of the clip, and click Cut. This will remove the effect from the clip.*

Step 5: Add Audio to Your Movie

Once you have placed clips on the storyboard, trimmed clips, and added transitions as desired, you can add audio to your movie. For example, you can add narration, background music, or even additional background noise—if it's an audio file, you can add it to your movie.

You may wonder, "What if I want to keep the audio on my existing video?" For example, let's say you tape a family reunion. Everyone is talking and laughing, but you want to add soft background music to the movie. Can you add the music without ruining the original audio? Absolutely! In this section, under Edit I'll show you how.

Adding Audio

If you switch to the Timeline view, you'll see an Audio/Music section on the timeline. You can drag music clips to this area to use in your video. (Remember that you import audio files in the same way that you import photos and video clips.) The following illustration shows the timeline with an audio clip added.

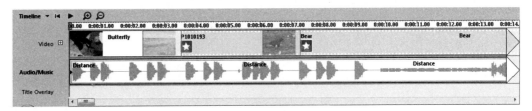

Just like trimming a video clip, you can drag the audio file on the timeline to trim off the beginning or end, as shown in the following illustration. To adjust the level of the audio volume, click Tools | Audio Levels.

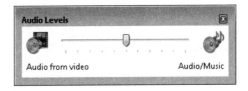

To record your voice, background music, or sounds, click Tools | Narrate Timeline. You should already have your computer microphone connected and tested, or make sure that any other sound input device that you want to use to record is ready.

To record an audio file:

1. Click Tools | Narrate Timeline. A window opens above the workspace, listing the sound device that you will use to record the audio. If you have more than one sound device installed on your computer, use the drop-down menu to select the device you want to use.

2. When you are ready to record, click the Start Narration button.

3. When you are finished recording, name the file and save it. The file now appears in your workspace timeline.

Recording narration or other background music or sound does not erase the original video soundtrack—it simply adds another stream of sound to the existing movie.

Step 6: Add Titles and Credits to your Movie

You can easily add a title to the beginning of the movie, titles before or on a selected clip, and credits at the end of the movie. In the Tasks pane, under Edit, click Titles And Credits. Your workspace changes so that you can select the kind of title that you want to add. To create your title:

1. In the Tasks pane, click Titles And Credits.

2. In the window that opens, choose the kind of title that you want to add, such as a title at the beginning.

3. Type the desired title or credit in the box that appears, shown in the following illustration.

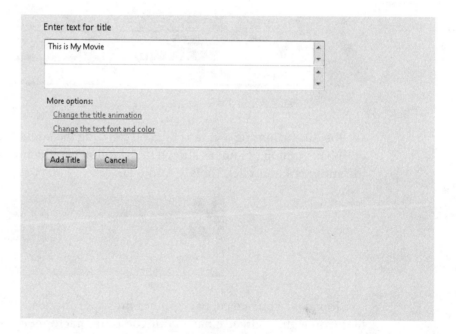

4. Play the clip with the title in the Monitor area, and view the animation and text font and color. Click the available link options just under your text, and make any desired changes, if necessary.

5. When you're done, click Add Title. Note that if you decided to use a title overlay so that a title rolls over a clip as it is playing, you can adjust the position of the overlay on the Title Overlay line in the Timeline view.

Step 7: Publishing Your Movie

Once you are finished with your movie, you can publish it. When you publish your movie, you can save it to your computer, burn it to a DVD or recordable CD, save it in a smaller format so you can e-mail it to someone, or you can record it back to your digital video camera.

In the Tasks pane, simply click the option you want, and follow the instructions to save the file. Note that if you choose to burn your movie to a DVD, the Windows DVD Maker appears. That's all there is to it.

Turn Windows Vista into a Media Center

What You'll Need

- **Windows Vista: Any version**
- **Cost: Free**

You've likely heard of Windows Media Center—after all, Windows Media Center first appeared as a PC you could purchase with an alternate operating system during the days of Windows XP. Windows Media Center was cool and useful, but many of us wanted a more conventional computer system and shied away from it.

Welcome to Windows Vista! Windows Vista has an integrated Media Center, which is really nice and, frankly, a feature you might miss if you're not careful. Media Center is easy to use. You can spend a little time with it and get the hang of it quickly. In this project, I'll introduce you to Media Center—you'll see what is available and how to access its different features. My bet is that after you read this project, Media Center will become a tool that you use time and time again.

Step 1: Open Media Center and Check Out the Options

Since Media Center is a built-in part of Windows Vista, you'll find it in Start | All Programs | Windows Media Center. When you first start the Media Center, you'll see a Welcome screen asking you to set it up. This "setup" routine will only take a minute as Media Center downloads files from the Internet, so go ahead and choose Express Setup and then click OK, shown in Figure 13-1.

Once you've set up Media Center, you will see the Start page, shown in Figure 13-2. If you point to the center selection area, you will see a scrolling down arrow. This allows you to flip through all of the available features in Media Center. While you're doing this, look to the right. Notice the right arrow. This selection arrow enables you to scroll through the options for whatever feature you've selected. Using these two arrows, you can access just about anything that you want in Media Center.

Figure 13-1

Choose the Express
Setup option.

Review the available options using the DOWN ARROW key and then click the
Settings button. This will take you to a general settings page for the different features

Figure 13-2

Choose what you
want to do from
the Start page.

you use in Media Center, such as TV, Pictures, Music, and so forth. If you click
a category, you can choose additional sub-categories to access additional settings. For
example, in Figure 13-3, I am looking at the general settings for startup and window
behavior. A few settings are selected by default, but you can enable some others as
well, if you want. Click through the different settings and categories to get a feel for
how Media Center is configured, and make any desired changes. Naturally, you may

Figure 13-3

Use Settings options to make changes.

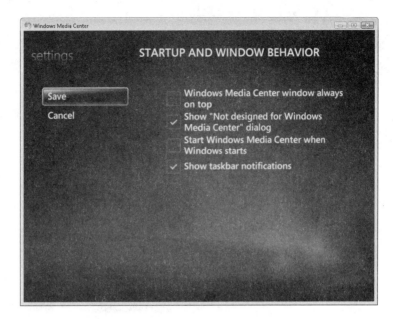

want to return to the setting options once you use Media Center's features a bit more and make additional changes.

Step 2: Use the Pictures + Video Feature

The Pictures + Video feature enables you to look at and use a picture library and/or a video library. Essentially, each feature gives you a way to look at and use your media. Let's consider each option in the next two sections.

View the Picture Library

If you select the Pictures + Video option on the Start page, you can then click the Picture Library to get started. When you first select the Picture Library, you will be prompted to add other folders to the library from your computer (such as personal photo folders and such). Follow the screen prompts to do this. Once you're done, you can look at your library of photos in three different views:

- **Folders** This view shows you the folders of photos on your PC. Click a folder to open it and view the photos or subfolders. This is the default view selected.

- **Tags** You can also view photos by tags, shown in the following illustration. If photos have been tagged with names and keywords in Windows Photo Gallery, those tags show up in Media Center, and you can browse your photo collection by keywords.

- **Date taken**   You can click the Date Taken option to see photos in the library sorted by date.

Aside from taking a look at your collection, you can also click the Play Slide Show button to see all of your photos as a slide show, shown in Figure 13-4. If you move your mouse to the lower-right corner, you can access standard controls that let you manually move around in the slide show.

Figure 13-4

Slide show feature

You can make some changes to the way that the slide show plays. Go back to the Settings menu and choose Pictures. Then scroll through the list of options. Choose transition times, types, whether to play music during the slide show, and so on. These settings are self-explanatory.

View the Video Library

The Video Library option works the same way as the Photo Library. You can open the Video Library and see videos according to folders or by the date they were taken. Then you can simply click the video that you want to see.

Step 3: Use Music in Media Center

If you click the Music option on the Start page, you can access the Music Library, Internet radio, or use a search feature to find the music you are looking for. As with all things in Media Center, these options are easy to use.

If you open the Music Library, you will see all of the music that is in the library in Windows Media Player. Thus, use Media Player to add items to the library. You can then use Media Center to look through your library and start playing songs or playlists. As you can see in Figure 13-5, you can look for music based on album title, artist, genre, song, playlist, or composer in much the same way you can look for songs within Media Player.

Figure 13-5

Use the Music Library to look through songs and playlists.

If you choose the album feature and select an album, you'll see options to play the album, add music from the album to the queue, burn the album to a CD, edit the album's information, or delete it from the library. You can also locate individual songs and add them to the queue.

You can also access and listen to radio stations on the Internet. While you're listening to music, you can see a visualization on the screen for entertainment purposes, much as you would with Windows Media Player. Turn on the visualization feature and choose a visualization by accessing the Settings feature and then choosing the Music category.

Step 4: Access Now Playing and the Queue

You can use the Start page to access the Now Playing area and view what songs you have added to the queue. Now Playing will show you what album or song is playing at the moment and allow you to access the queue, turn on a visualization, play a slide show at the same time, and use shuffle and repeat controls, as shown in Figure 13-6.

If you click the View Queue option, you can see what songs are in the queue, edit it, clear songs, and even create a playlist from the songs you have in the queue. Just click the relevant button to access the feature you want.

Figure 13-6

Now Playing area

Step 5: Use Other Features

In addition to these primary features, you can access a few other options within the Media Center. Here's a quick list to get you started:

- **TV and Movies** You can watch TV and movies using Media Center. See Project 14 to learn more about these features.

- **Online Media**   Use this option to access any online media configured for use on your computer, such as online games, online music, radio, movies, pictures, and news.

- **Access Tasks**   Use this option to lock Media Center, shut down Media Center, burn a CD or DVD, or sync up with other devices. You can also add extenders so that you can use other devices and services with Media Center, such as Xbox and third-party products.

Watch TV on Windows Vista

What You'll Need

- Windows Vista: Any version
- TV tuner card
- Cost: $100 or less

I f your PC running Windows Vista has a TV tuner card, you can watch and record television on Windows Vista. Why, you might ask? The answer is simple. With Windows Vista, you can not only watch live TV, you can also record television and watch it at a later time or, even better, you can pause live television and "catch up" to your favorite program when you return. With Windows Media Center and Windows Vista, you are truly in control of your television-viewing experience.

Naturally, Windows Vista will play CDs, and you can watch DVD movies, but with a television connection, you can quickly find your favorite shows, watch them, record them, and pause them when you need to step away. In this project, you'll see how to use Windows Vista to make your television-viewing experience a blast.

Step 1: Purchase a TV Tuner Card

You'll use Windows Media Center to watch and record live television (find out more about Media Center in Project 13), but before you can do that, you'll need to purchase and install a TV tuner card. If you purchased a Windows Media Center–based PC, you may already have a TV tuner card, but the odds are that you'll need to purchase and install one. Check your PC's documentation for more information.

Most TV tuner cards are PCI cards, meaning that that the device attaches to an internal slot on your computer. TV tuner cards typically cost between 50 and 100 dollars, and you'll be able to find one at your local computer store, or you can shop online at Windows Marketplace, which you can access from the Welcome Center in Windows Vista (click Start | Windows Vista).

You'll need to follow the information that comes with the card concerning installation. Once the card is installed correctly, just attach your cable television to the card and you're all set!

Step 2: Set Up the TV Tuner in Media Center

The first thing you'll need to do is allow Media Center to configure the TV tuner. Click Start | Windows Media Center. On the Start page, scroll to select TV + Movies, and then choose the Set Up TV option, shown in Figure 14-1. Media Center will configure itself to work with the television, so simply follow any prompts that appear. If Windows Media Center cannot locate your TV tuner card, you'll see a message telling you so. In this case, you'll need to check the instructions about installing your card again.

Figure 14-1

Set up television viewing in Media Center.

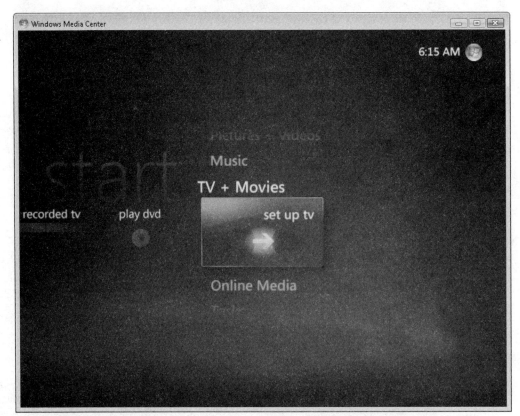

Step 3: Finding Movies on TV

Once Media Center is set up for television, you'll see a Movie Guide option when you access TV + Movies on the Start page. You can use the guide to search for movies on your television channels by rating, by what is currently on, by what is on next, or by genre. Once you find a movie that you want to view, just click Watch.

For a narrower search, click TV + Movies on the Start page, and click Search. Using the Search window, you can look for movies by title, keywords, categories, actors, or even directors. The search will give you movies that are currently playing, as well as future showings.

Step 4: Watching and Pausing Live TV

To watch live TV, click TV + Movies on the Start page, and click Live TV. You can see information about the program you are watching by right-clicking the TV show and clicking Program Info. Click Watch to return to the program.

As with any music or movie playback in Media Center, you'll see a control bar at the bottom of your screen (just hover your mouse there to make it appear if you don't see it). You can use the controls to adjust the volume and even change the channel. If you have a PC running Windows Media Center, you can also use your remote control for this purpose. When you're not using the controls, they disappear from sight, giving you a true TV experience without any visual interruptions. Figure 14-2 shows you an example of how a movie looks when played on Windows Vista.

Figure 14-2

Watching TV on Windows Vista.

Let's say you're in the middle of your favorite show and someone comes to the door. You can avoid missing your show by simply pausing live TV. When you pause live TV, Windows Vista records the show to a file. When you return, you can start watching where you left off until you eventually catch back up with the live TV. You can do all of this without jumping through a bunch of configuration hoops or anything like that.

When you want to pause live TV, press the Pause button on the control bar. When you want to continue watching, click the Play button. You can use the Fast Forward or Rewind buttons as well. This way, you can simply fast-forward through commercials until you catch back up with live TV. It's that simple! You never have to worry about finding the files Windows Vista creates to record your paused television—just come back and enjoy!

Step 5: Recording and Using Play Back

While watching television in Windows Vista can be helpful due to the ability to pause live TV, you can also record a show or movie and watch it later. You can record a show or movie that is playing at the moment, or you can choose one that will play at a later time and record it.

note *Unfortunately, you can't record one show and watch another at the same time. In order to do this, you would need at least two TV tuners installed on your PC—one to record the show and one to watch the different show. This is a limitation of the TV tuner. You can find out more about using multiple TV tuners on your PC running Windows Vista by accessing Windows Help.*

To record a movie or show that is currently playing, just start watching the show or movie and click the Record button on the control bar that appears at the bottom of your screen. This is a great way to record the rest of a show or movie if you start watching it but get interrupted.

If you want to record a show or movie that has not aired yet, you have a few options you'll enjoy:

- Access the Movie Guide to record an entire series. Just right-click the series, and click Record Series.

- To record by channel or time, click TV + Movies and click Recorded TV. Click Add Recording, and then click Channel And Time. Enter the channel and time information or start and stop times, and then click Record.

- To record only the new episodes of a series, access the Start page and choose Tasks | Settings | TV | Recorder, and then click Recording Defaults. Under Series Only Recording Defaults, select First Run to record only shows that have an original air date of less than a week and that are not marked as reruns.

After you record a show or movie, you can access TV + Movies and then access recorded TV. Here, you'll see a list of movies or shows that have been recorded, as you can see in Figure 14-3. You can look through your list of movies or shows by the date they were recorded or by title.

To play a movie or show, click it, and you'll see a Movie Details screen, shown in Figure 14-4. Click Play to start playing the movie, or you can get more information about the movie, delete it, or burn it to a CD or DVD.

Figure 14-3

Recorded TV

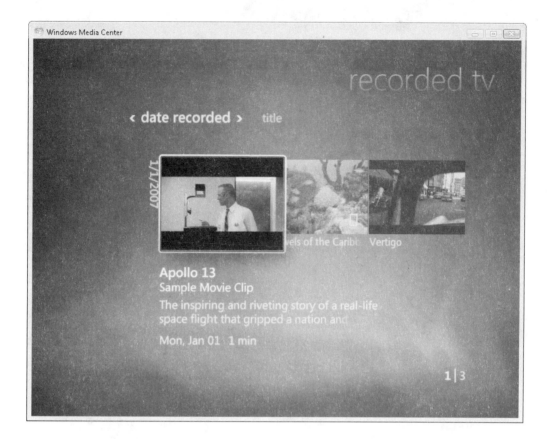

Figure 14-4

Movie details

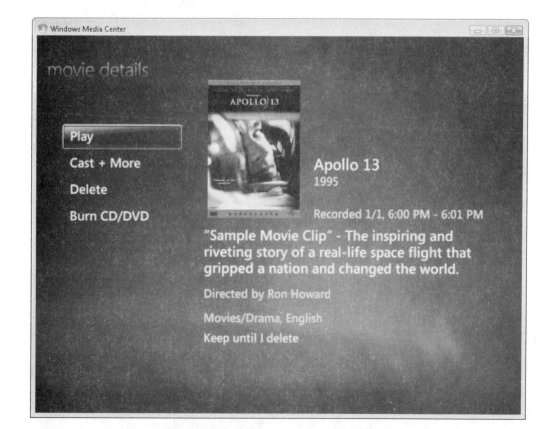

Project 15
Talk to Windows Vista

What You'll Need

- **Windows Vista: Any version**
- **Special hardware required: Microphone**
- **Cost: $40 or less**

Imagine the day when keyboards do not exist. A day when you simply talk to your computer and it does what you ask. If that sounds more like an episode of *Star Trek* than reality, think again. In the computing world, the concept of "human interface" when it comes to computers is highly important. The idea is that computers should communicate in the same way that humans do. Although we're not there yet, computer technology has come a long way in the past few years, and speech recognition software has become much better. Windows Vista includes a new speech tool that enables you to set up Windows Vista so that you can give it voice commands and it can read text back to you. In this project, you'll see how to set up this cool feature so that you can talk to Windows Vista—at least some of the time.

Step 1: Purchase a Microphone

Before you get started, you'll need a microphone in order to be able to communicate with your computer. If you visit your local computer or discount store, you'll find all kinds of microphones at various costs. First, you need to make sure that the microphone you purchase is compatible with Windows Vista. Check the microphone's box for compatibility information.

Next, you'll need to determine the style you want, such as a free-standing mike that sits on your desk or a headset microphone that you wear. The decision is completely yours.

Finally, install the microphone on Windows Vista. Attach the mike to the computer, and follow any installation instructions that come with it. In most cases, all you'll need to do is attach the microphone, turn it on, and Windows Vista will automatically detect and install it.

Step 2: Check Your Microphone's Settings

Now that your microphone is installed, you should check the settings and make sure that everything is in good working order. This will only take a moment. First, right-click the Sound icon in the notification area, and click Recording Devices. In the dialog box that appears, shown in Figure 15-1, you see the recording devices attached to your computer. Select the one you want to use, and click the Properties button.

Figure 15-1

Recording devices installed on your computer.

The Properties dialog box appears. Click the Levels tab, and adjust the microphone input level. A setting around 50 is typically a good setting, as you can see in Figure 15-2.

Step 3: Configure Speech Recognition

As I mentioned, speech recognition is a cool feature of Windows Vista, and Control Panel even gives you a Speech Recognition Options applet, with several choices to help you get started. First, click Start | Control Panel | Speech Recognition Options. You see a window with several options, as shown in Figure 15-3.

1. Click the Start Speech Recognition option, and a wizard appears to walk you through the process. Read the introductory information, and click Next on the Welcome screen.

Figure 15-2

Adjust the
microphone level.

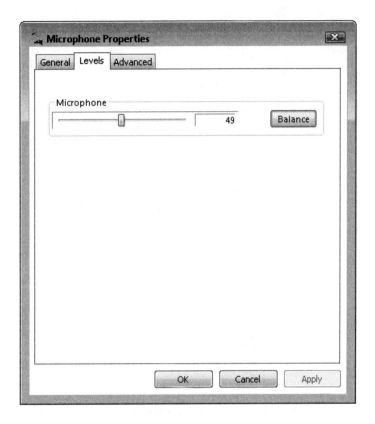

Figure 15-3

Speech recognition
options

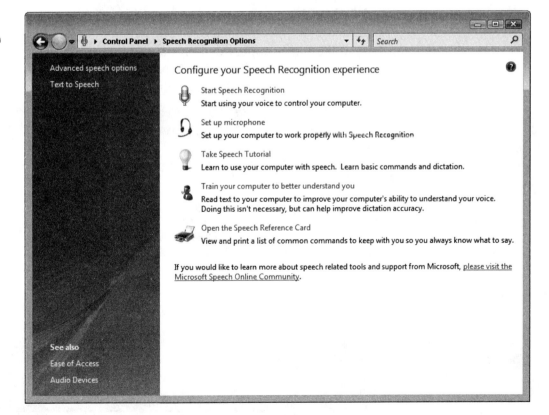

2. In the next window, shown in the following illustration, choose the kind of microphone that you'll be using, such as a headset, desktop, or other if you're using a mike that is built into another device. Click Next.

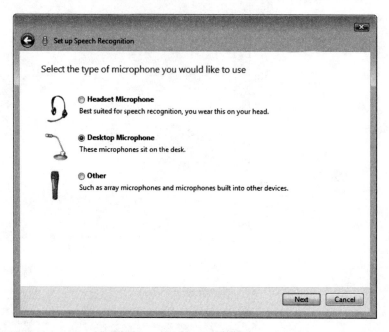

3. The next window gives you some basic information about microphone placement. Review this information carefully, and click Next when you're done.

4. Windows Vista will now adjust your microphone level by having you read a sentence to the computer. Use your microphone as instructed in step 3, and read the sentence provided on the screen, shown in the following illustration. When you're done, click Next and then follow any additional instructions that appear. Click Next again.

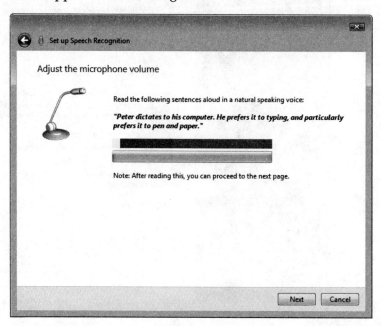

5. At this point, you see an option to improve speech recognition accuracy. This feature allows speech recognition to review documents and e-mail in order to better understand words and phrases you use so that it can identify them when you speak. The information in your documents and e-mail help the computer learn your "language"—this information is not sent to Microsoft or to other users. You should enable document review, and then click Next.

6. Next, you can print the speech reference card, which is a list of commands that the computer can respond to. You can click the View button to view the reference sheet and print it. If you want to do this later, it is available as an option any time you open Speech Recognition Options in Control Panel. However, you'll need this card, so it's probably best to print it now. Make your selection and click Next.

7. Next, choose if you want to start Speech Recognition every time you start your computer. Click Next.

8. Finally, you have the option to walk through a speech recognition tutorial that will help you understand more about talking to Windows Vista. The tutorial may help you solve problems and understand speech recognition better. You can click Start Tutorial to begin. Your computer is now configured for speech recognition.

Step 4: Using Speech Recognition

Now that speech recognition is turned on and working, you can begin using it. You talk to your computer, giving it commands and instructions, as noted in the reference card. As mentioned, you should print the reference card and keep it near you. Since speech recognition is now turned on, you'll see a speech recognition control box on your desktop. By default, speech recognition is "sleeping," which means it does not respond to voice commands, as shown in the following illustration. You can turn on speech recognition by saying "Start listening" into your microphone and turn it off at any time by saying "Stop listening."

Once you tell speech recognition to start listening, you'll see that the control says "Listening." Windows Vista is now ready to respond to voice commands, as you can see in the following illustration.

If you say something that Windows Vista doesn't understand, the control will respond with "What was that?" as you can see in the following information. At this point, you need to repeat your command.

Spend a few minutes giving Windows Vista some voice commands, and see how your computer responds. Remember to use the reference card for help and additional instructions.

Step 6: Train Windows Vista to Understand You Better

I live in Texas, so my "proper" use of English language and pronunciation isn't always accurate. Now, before you pass judgment, the odds are good that you have certain pronunciation issues as well, no matter where you live!

The good news is that you can train Windows Vista to better understand you. Once you set up speech recognition, you should walk through this process to help Windows Vista understand you better and cut down your personal frustration.

Click Start | Control Panel | Speech Recognition Options. In the window that opens, click Train Your Computer To Better Understand You or, if speech recognition is turned on, you can say this command sequence aloud.

This starts a series of steps, where you will read different sentences, as you can see in the following illustration. When the training session is done, just click or say "Finish."

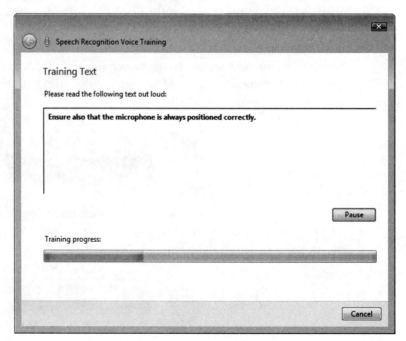

Project 16

Synchronize Your Vista PC with Other Computers and Devices

What You'll Need

- Windows Vista: Any version
- A home network
- Cost: Free

Most of us have data we just can't live without. I have a folder of information that contains a lot of important documents and files. I keep that folder on my laptop, but I also have a copy of it on another computer just for safe-keeping. Then, I also back up the laptop so that there's another copy. The problem, of course, is that the information in this folder changes often, so if I'm not careful, I end up with multiple copies of the same folder on different computers—none of which have the most up-to-date information.

With Windows Vista, I can avoid all of these issues using a new tool called the Sync Center. You can use the Sync Center to keep your files and other information "in sync" between your computer, another computer, mobile devices, network folders, and even between compatible programs. In this project, you'll discover how to use this helpful tool.

 The ability to sync with network folders is not included in Windows Vista Start, Home Basic, or Home Premium editions.

Step 1: Open the Sync Center

Sync, which stands for synchronization, enables you to keep data the same that is contained in several computers or devices. In the past, the synchronization process was complicated to set up and use—so much so that most people didn't try it. The good news is that the Sync Center in Windows Vista is easy to use and you don't have to worry about complicated settings—Windows Vista can handle those for you.

You access the Sync Center by clicking Start | All Programs | Accessories | Sync Center. Initially, you'll see a typical Windows folder with nothing in it, shown in Figure 16-1. You have to set up a Sync Partnership first. We'll do that in the next step.

Figure 16-1

Sync Center

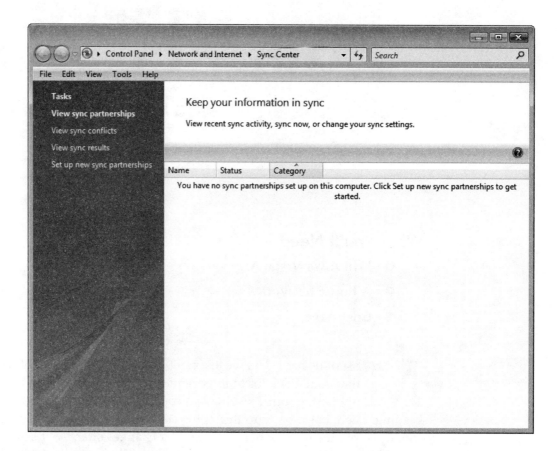

tip   *You can get to Sync Center and other accessories and tools more quickly by clicking Start and typing "sync" in the Search box. The Sync Center option will appear immediately on the Start menu. Try this feature as you access programs and data in Windows Vista.*

Step 2: Set Up a Sync Partnership

In order to sync with a device or other computer, you need to make sure the device is connected to your computer running Windows Vista, such as through a wireless connection, Universal Serial Bus (USB) cable, or however you normally connect the device. Then you're ready to set up what is known as a sync partnership.

In the Sync Center, click Set Up New Sync Partnerships in the left pane. The Sync Center will scan your computer for devices for possible sync relationships and list them in the Sync Center. As you can see in Figure 16-2, I not only have a device connected to my PC, but also a network folder.

Figure 16-2

Establish sync partnerships.

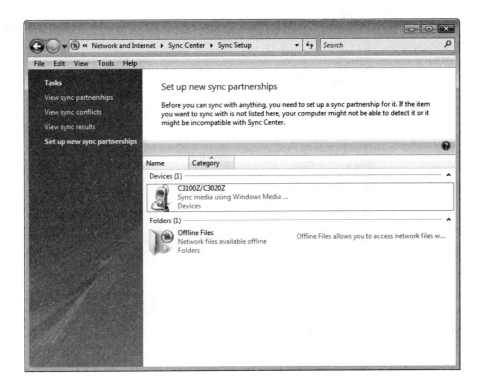

> **tip** *If you have a device connected to your computer running Windows Vista that does not appear in the list for possible sync partnerships, there is likely a problem with the device's compatibility with Windows Vista. Refer to the Windows Help file for more information about device compatibility.*

Now that you have a listing of possible sync partnerships, you can set them up. Select the device that you want to set up for a sync partnership, and a Set Up button appears on the small toolbar above the listing. Click the Set Up button. Depending on what you are syncing with, you'll see a different window, where you can select what you want to sync, how often, and if the sync should be automatic. For example, in Figure 16-3, I am synching playlists with a device.

Step 3: Manage Sync Partnerships

Once you set up a sync partnership with a device or network folder, there isn't much you need to do if you have allowed the sync partnership to be an automatic one. You can sync manually by selecting the device and clicking Sync on the toolbar. You can also look under Tasks in the left pane of the Sync Center and view sync partnerships, conflicts, and results. These are especially helpful if you believe that there may be a problem with the Sync Center in terms of a sync partnership.

Figure 16-3

Set up synchronization
with a device.

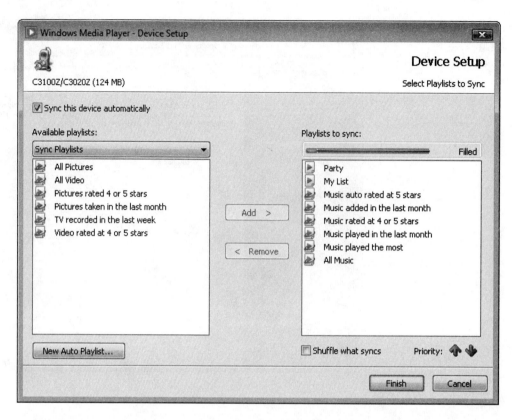

If you believe there may be a problem, or if you at least want to view the contents
of the device before you start syncing, you may be able to right-click the device's listing
in Sync Center and click Explore to see the current contents. However, not all devices
support the Explore feature, so you have to access those devices directly through the
Computer or Network applets in Control Panel to see their current contents.

Step 4: Resolving a Sync Conflict

From time to time, a sync conflict may occur, which you can see if you click View Sync
Conflicts in the left console pane. A sync conflict occurs when the file Windows Vista is
trying to sync with has changed in two different locations. In this case, Windows Vista
doesn't know which file is the most current and will need your assistance to choose.

For example, let's say that you have a playlist on your computer and an MP3
player. The two are synchronized. However, you make changes to the playlist on your
MP3 player, but you also make some different changes to the playlist on Windows
Vista. When you start to sync them, Windows Vista will not know which version of
the playlist should be used because they have both changed, creating a conflict.

In this case, you get to determine how the sync conflict should be resolved. In the
Sync Center, click the View Sync Conflicts option, and you'll see the conflict listed in
the Sync Center. Select the conflict and click the Resolve button on the toolbar. The
Sync Center will give you the details of the conflict so that you can choose how to
resolve it. Just follow the instructions that appear.

Step 5: Resolving a Sync Error

In some cases, a sync error will occur due to incompatibility with devices or, in the case of network folders, a network problem, server problem, or an access problem. Whatever the case, you can click View Sync Results in the Tasks pane and see a listing of errors, warnings, or other sync information that may be available.

As you can see in Figure 16-4, I have a listing of errors. All of these errors occurred because I attempted to sync with a network folder for which I do not have access. For each warning, error, or other problem, I can select one and click the Properties button to learn more about the nature of the problem, in which case, I can try and troubleshoot the problem after gaining some information. Note that the Sync Center will not solve these problems for you, but it will give you information so that you can resolve them.

Figure 16-4

Sync errors

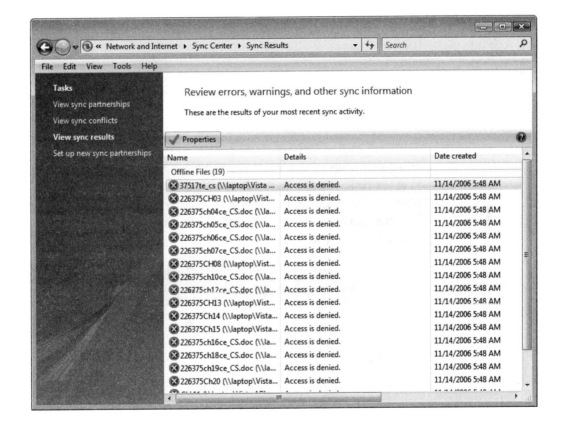

Step 6: Establishing a Sync Schedule

Once you establish a sync partnership (and deal with any problems or errors), you can establish a sync schedule so that the device or network folder is synced as often as you like.

In the Sync Center, select the sync partnership you want to schedule, and click the Schedule button that appears on the toolbar. On the Items window that opens, shown in the following illustration, choose the item you want to schedule, and click Next.

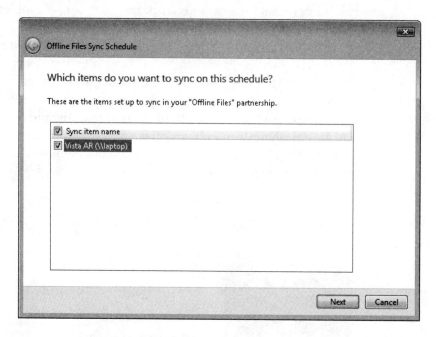

Next, choose when you want the sync to begin. You have the ability to create a scheduled time, or you can trigger the sync for when an event or action occurs, such as every time you log on to your computer or the network. If you choose a scheduled time, you will see a schedule window, where you can choose when you want the sync to occur and how often the sync should repeat, as shown in the following illustration. The options here are self-explanatory.

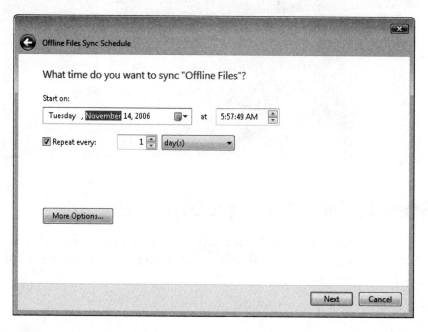

If you choose the action or event option, you can choose different sync starting options, such as when you log on, when the computer is idle, or when you lock or unlock Windows. Just make your selection, and click Next.

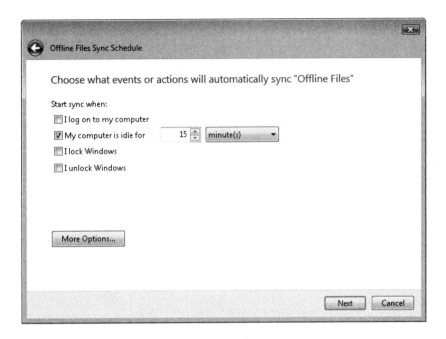

If at any time you want to change the sync schedule that you have created, just select the sync partnership in the Sync Center, and click the Schedule button on the toolbar again. You'll see the option to create a different schedule, view or edit the existing one, or delete the existing schedule.

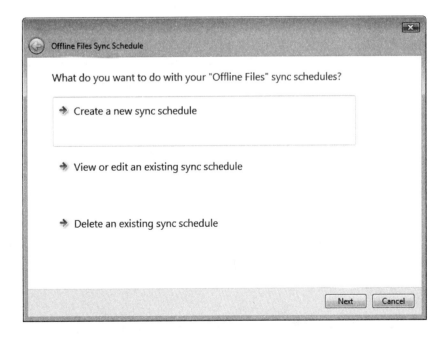

Eliminate Spam and Unwanted Messages in Windows Mail

What You'll Need

- **Windows Vista: Any version**
- **Cost: Free**

I use e-mail all of the time. I check it first thing when I get up in the morning. I sometimes think back to only a few years ago when e-mail was mostly unheard of and ignored, and I wonder how I survived. Today, millions upon millions of e-mail messages are sent every day, and naturally, millions of junk e-mail messages, spam, and phishing e-mail messages are sent as well. From medications without a prescription to spoofed e-mail that looks like eBay telling you to enter your account information, junk e-mail is really annoying. The good news is that Windows Vista includes a new e-mail program called Windows Mail with features that can help you greatly reduce the amount of junk e-mail you receive. These features should make your e-mail experience more enjoyable and less frustrating, so let's get started!

Step 1: Choose a Junk Mail Safety Level

Windows Mail enables you to choose a protection level for junk e-mail. This helpful feature keeps you in control of your e-mail by allowing you to choose how "strong" you want the junk mail filter to be on your system. Your first step in protecting yourself against junk e-mail is to choose a setting that is right for you.

If you click Tools | Junk E-mail Options in Windows Mail, you'll see a Junk E-mail Options windows with an Options tab, shown in Figure 17-1. On the Options tab, you need to choose from the following list the level of junk e-mail protection that you want to use.

- **No Automatic Filtering**   If you choose this option, Windows Mail doesn't do anything with junk e-mail except move any blocked senders to the Junk E-mail folder. In other words, if you don't tell Windows Mail to block a particular sender, Windows Mail does nothing to protect you.

- **Low**   With this setting, the most obvious pieces of junk e-mail are moved to the Junk E-mail folder. You'll still get a number of pieces of junk e-mail in your inbox with this setting.

- **High**   With this setting, most of the junk e-mail will be filtered and put in the Junk E-mail folder, but some e-mail you want may get filtered as well. If you use this setting, you'll need to regularly check the Junk E-mail folder to make sure that no wanted e-mail ends up there.

- **Safe List Only**   Only e-mail from people or domains that you have added to your Safe list will appear in your inbox. This option is too restrictive for most users.

Notice also that you have a check box that allows you to permanently delete suspected junk e-mail instead of moving it to your Junk E-mail folder. I don't recommend using this setting because wanted e-mail messages could also get deleted if they are suspected junk mail. It's best to let Windows Mail move suspected junk e-mail to the Junk E-mail folder. You can then delete it from there when you know it is safe to do so.

Figure 17-1

Choose a security setting option.

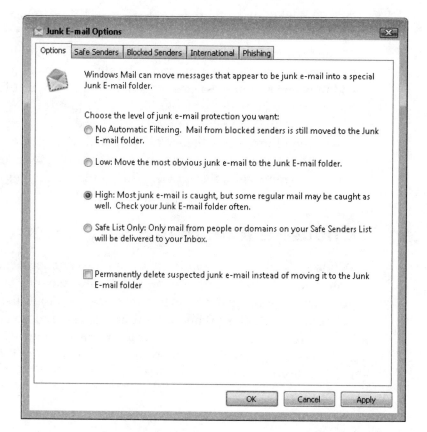

Step 2: Add Safe or Blocked Senders

If you click Tools | Junk E-mail Options, you'll notice a Safe Senders tab and a Blocked Senders tab. These tabs are exactly the same, except that one allows you to enter safe senders, while the other allows you to enter blocked senders, as you can see on the Blocked Senders tab shown in Figure 17-2. You don't need to enter every e-mail address or domain on the Safe Senders list, but it can be helpful to add certain e-mail addresses or domains that should never be blocked.

On the other hand, let's say that you seem to get a lot of mail from a particular e-mail address, perhaps someone you met in a chat room or other place on the Internet. If you no longer want to receive e-mail from this person, you can add the e-mail address to the Blocked Senders list. Now, every time you get an e-mail from this person, the e-mail is automatically moved to the Junk E-mail Options list.

To add a person to the Safe or Blocked Senders list, click the Add button on the appropriate tab, enter the e-mail address, and click OK. The e-mail address is now added. Naturally, you can return to the tab and change or remove the safe or blocked sender at any time.

Figure 17-2

Blocked Senders list

tip *If you receive an e-mail and you want to add the sender to your Blocked or Safe Senders list, select the message in your inbox, click Message | Junk E-mail, and choose to either add the sender to your Safe Senders list or block the sender.*

Step 3: Block International E-mail

Depending on where you live, you may want to block e-mail from certain international domains or languages. For example, if you know that you have no business receiving e-mail from the AL domain (Albania), or you don't speak or read Chinese and you have no business getting e-mail in that language, you can block these domains or languages so that relevant e-mail is automatically sent to the Junk E-mail folder. As you can see in Figure 17-3, the International tab (click Tools | Junk E-mail Options), helps you do just that.

Figure 17-3

International options

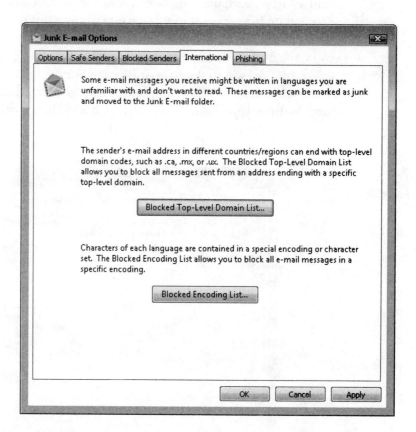

You can click either the Blocked Top-Level Domain List button or the Blocked Encoding List button (which is languages), and choose to block whatever domains or languages you want in the list provided (see Figure 17-4). Just select the desired check boxes, and click OK.

Step 4: Use the Phishing Filter

Phishing (pronounced "fishing") is a criminal's tool to get personally identifiable information, such as user names, passwords, bank accounts, credit card numbers, and so on, from you. It works like this: You receive an e-mail from what appears to be a valid company, such as eBay. The e-mail tells you there are problems with your account

Figure 17-4

Choose what you want to block.

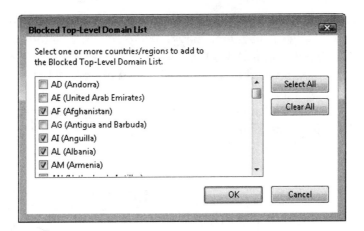

information and asks you to click a link to access a Web page, where you can update the information. You click the link, and the Web page looks legitimate. You enter your information, thinking it's a real Web site, but instead, it is a fake Web site designed to gather your information, which can then be used in unscrupulous ways. This trick is effective and it fools many people because the phishing e-mails look so real. For example, Figure 17-5 shows you an example of a phishing e-mail. Although the e-mail looks real, there are clues that it is not, as shown in the figure.

Figure 17-5

Sample phishing e-mail

Windows Mail can help reduce the amount of phishing e-mail you receive, but you should also always be wary of any e-mail that asks you for personal information, even if it appears that you are going to a legitimate Web site. If in doubt, leave the e-mail and surf directly to the site, such as www.ebay.com, and then contact customer service from there. They can help you know if the e-mail is legitimate. Never trust any kind of e-mail like this.

To use the phishing filter in Windows Mail, click Tools | Junk E-mail Options, click the Phishing tab, and choose to protect your inbox from phishing e-mail. It's also a good idea to automatically move phishing e-mail to the Junk E-mail folder, shown in Figure 17-6.

Figure 17-6

Protect yourself from phishing e-mail.

Step 5: Create a Message Rule

In some cases, you may want to create a message rule. Messages rules help you further identify junk e-mail and tell Windows Mail what to do with them, which is typically delete them. However, message rules can also be used in a positive way. Let's say you have a colleague at work who sends you a lot of mail. You want this mail to automatically go to a particular folder. You can create a message rule to handle that for you.

When you create a message rule, you determine a condition and an action for the rule. You can create as many message rules as you like, but you should have a specific goal in mind when you create one. Random and nonspecific rules may cause you more problems than they solve. To create a message rule:

I. Click Tools | Message Rules | Mail. The New Mail Rule dialog box appears, as shown in the following illustration.

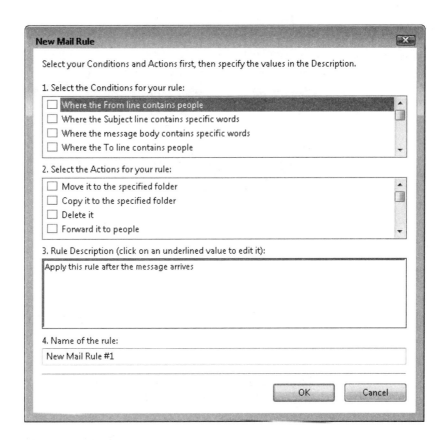

2. Choose a desired condition from the check boxes available. In this example, I am going to move e-mail from a particular person to a particular folder, so in the conditions area, I choose Where The From Line Contains People.

3. In the actions area, choose a desired action. I have chosen to move the e-mail to a specified folder.

4. In the Rule Description area, you see some underlined links, shown in the following illustration. Now that I have a condition and an action, I can click

each link and further configure the rule. First, I click the Contains People link so that I can enter who the "people" are for this rule.

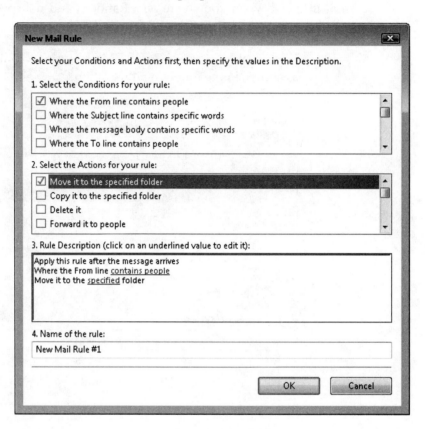

5. As you can see in the following illustration, I have added the colleague's name. Now, when ever I get e-mail from Jim Anderson, the rule will go into effect. I click OK when finished.

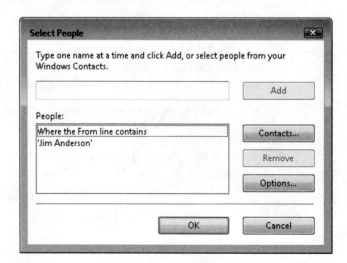

6. Now I'll configure the action for the rule. I click the rule option back on the New Mail Rule dialog box. Since I wanted to move Jim's e-mail to a specified folder, I have created a folder in Windows Mail and selected it for the target folder, shown in the following illustration. Now, all of Jim's e-mail to me will automatically be placed in this folder instead of in my inbox. I click OK when finished.

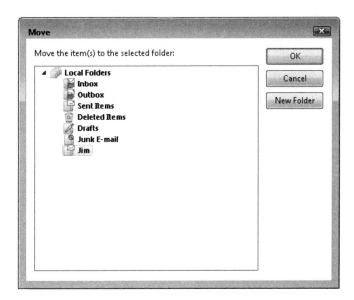

7. Click OK on the New Mail Rule dialog box. The new mail rule now goes into effect. Naturally, I can go back and change this rule at any time.

Part III

Advanced

Improve Your Computer's Performance

What You'll Need

- **Windows Vista: Any version**
- **Cost: Free**

Don't skip this project. Unless you are a computer junkie, the idea of improving your computer's performance may sound boring at the least. You're probably thinking it entails tweaking some settings here and there and stuff like that. While some of that may be true, you'll miss out on some new Windows Vista features that tell you exactly how your computer ranks and helps you improve your ranking if you don't pay attention to your computer's performance. If you're a game player, this project can be critical for you, because Windows Vista's new tools really outline exactly what your computer is capable of handling—and what it's not. So, work through this project with me and let's find out if your PC has the right stuff or if it needs some work!

Step 1: Access Performance Information and Tools

You'll find the new performance tools and goodies by clicking Start | Control Panel | Performance Information And Tools (make sure Control Panel is in Classic View). Or, you can click Start and type "performance" in the Search box. Performance Information And Tools will appear as a clickable link on the Start menu.

Either way, you arrive at the Performance Information And Tools window, shown in Figure 18-1. First things first, you'll notice that your computer has been given a score. My score at present is 3.0. This score is called the Windows Experience Index, and it is a measurement of the capability of your computer's hardware and software to handle the demands of modern computing. Your final score is called your "base score" because it is based on the lowest score among all of your components. Notice that in Figure 18-1 the components on my system received a subscore. My lowest subscore is the gaming graphics, which was given a 3.0. So my final score is determined by my lowest subscore.

Figure 18-1

Performance informa-
tion and tools

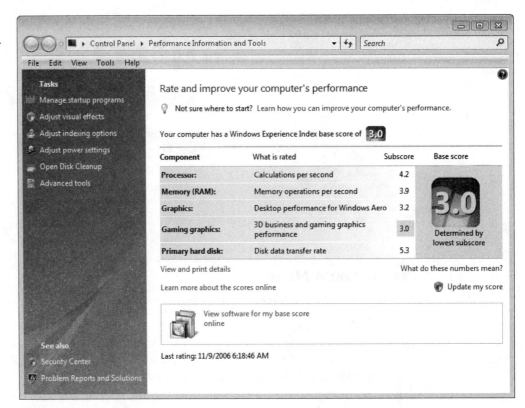

Scores can range from 1 to 6, so the scores you see give you an overall idea of your computer's component scores. The cool thing is that you can view and print the details of the score by clicking the View And Print Details link, and you can also view software appropriate for your base score online at Windows Marketplace. Software is rated so that you can check its necessary base score against yours to see if your computer is powerful enough to run the software.

All you have at this point is information—although it is certainly good information. The next task, then, is to use Windows Vista to improve some of the performance options you see here. Note that some improvements can only be made with a hardware upgrade. For example, my lowest scores have to do with gaming graphics and graphics in general. Although a score of 3.0 is not bad, it is not great if I want to play games and use 3D applications. In this case, there is nothing I can do except upgrade my computer's graphics card to improve this score.

However, you can access the Tools features under Tasks to help improve the general performance of your computer, so let's take a quick look at your options and how to use them in the next sections.

Step 2: Manage Startup Programs

Startup programs are exactly what you might think—they are the programs that start when your start your computer. It's great to have some programs do that, but if you have too many of them starting up, they can slow down your boot time. In addition, you don't want any programs open and running that you don't intend on using because they can consume system resources that could be used for something else.

In the Performance Information And Tools window, click the Manage Startup Programs link in the Tasks pane. This opens Windows Defender, where the Software Explorer page shows you the startup programs, shown in Figure 18-2. Notice that you can select a program and click the Disable button to stop the program from starting when you start Windows. For example, speech recognition starts when I start Windows, but I can stop this behavior by selecting it in the list and clicking the Disable button.

Figure 18-2

Manage startup programs

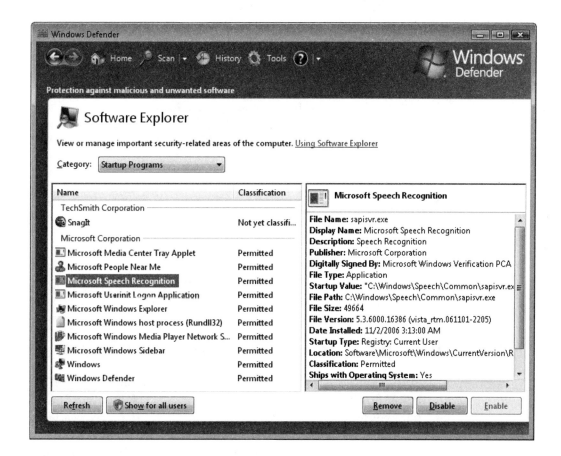

Step 3: Adjust the Visual Effects

As you are probably well aware at this point, your computer must meet certain hardware requirements to use the Aero interface. You can check to see if Aero is enabled on your PC or if it is even an option for you by accessing Personalization in Control Panel.

However, you can also reduce the demand on your graphics card and processor by clicking Adjust Visual Effects in the Tasks list. This will open the Performance Options dialog box, see Figure 18-3, where you can adjust the visual effects in Windows for the best appearance or performance. By default, the options on the Visual Effects tab are set for allowing Windows to choose what's best. However, you can choose a different option, and you can even customize what you see in Windows, by clicking the Custom option and then selecting or clearing the relevant check boxes.

Figure 18-3

Adjust visual effects.

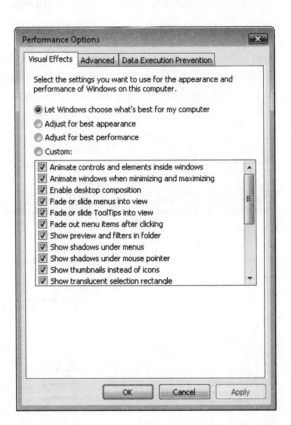

Step 4: Adjust Indexing Options and Power Settings

You'll notice indexing options and power settings links in the Tasks pane. You can adjust how your computer indexes information for searches and what power settings your computer is using. For the most part, I'm not convinced that either of these settings will have a big impact on performance, so I wouldn't worry much about them. The power settings option is something you should check just to make sure that your computer is set to conserve power in a way that matches how you work and play with Windows Vista. If you click the power settings feature, you'll be able to select from a balanced, power saver, or high performance plan, as shown in Figure 18-4. You can also adjust individual settings for each by clicking the Change Plan Settings link.

Figure 18-4

Power options

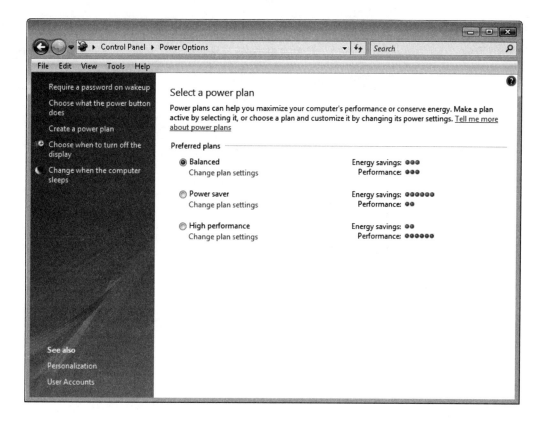

Step 5: Use Disk Cleanup

Disk Cleanup is not a new tool in Windows Vista—it's been around in the past several versions of Windows. However, it remains an important tool, because computers tend to pick up a lot of junk, especially if you're an Internet hog. You should run Disk Cleanup every month or so and get rid of any unnecessary information on your system, thus freeing up more storage space for things you really want.

When you click Disk Cleanup in Tasks, you'll be prompted to choose to clean up your files or entire computer and then choose a drive to clean up. Then you can choose what kinds of files you want to delete, shown in Figure 18-5. It's always a good idea to get rid of temporary Internet files and items you've already put in the Recycle Bin. Just make your selections and then click OK to clean up the disk.

Step 6: Use Advanced Tools

If you click Advanced Tools in Tasks, you'll see an Advanced Tools window with a listing of the items available to you, shown in Figure 18-6. There are some cool new tools here that you can play around with, and you'll also find some tried and true tools from previous versions of Windows.

The following sections give you a quick look at the tools and what they do.

Figure 18-5

Disk Cleanup

Figure 18-6

Advanced tool options

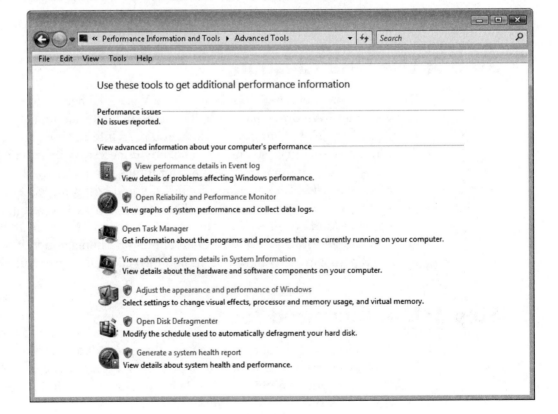

Event Log

The Event Log tool is an older tool (a bit refurbished in Windows Vista) that gives you information about system events and errors. Event Log doesn't do anything to help you resolve any problems, but it is a great way to gather information about issues your computer might have so that you can then troubleshoot the problem. You should check Event Log from time to time just to get an idea about any possible issues with your PC.

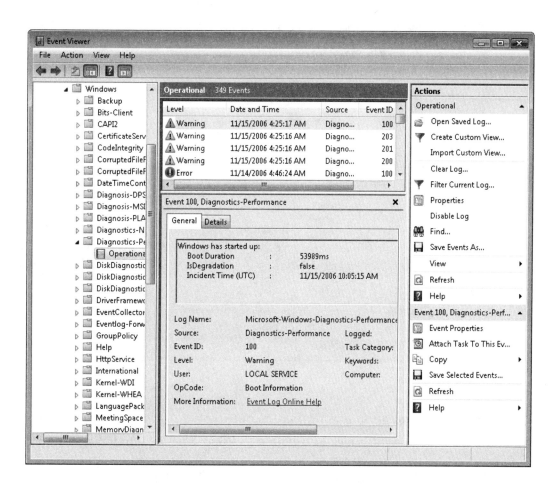

Reliability And Performance Monitor

This tool is a revamp of the old Performance Monitor that has been around in Windows for years. This one is easier to use, but still rather complicated. You can create monitoring events and view a stability chart under the Reliability Monitor, shown in the following illustration. Though a discussion of it is beyond the scope of this book, the Reliability And Performance Monitor can be a great troubleshooting tool if your computer is having performance problems. You can learn more about how to use the features here in Windows Help.

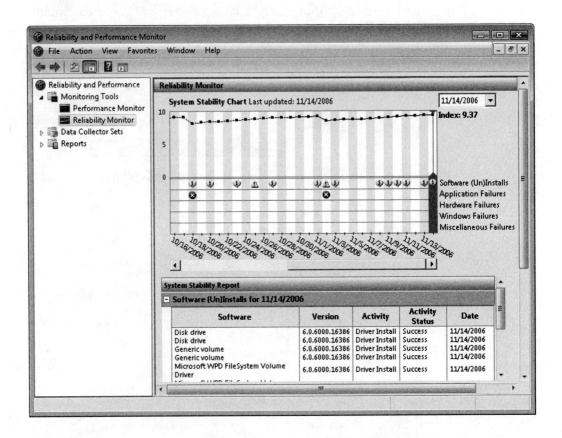

Task Manager

Task Manager is certainly nothing new in Windows Vista either, but it remains an important tool to manage running applications, processes, and services. It also has a Performance tab, shown in the following illustration, where you can see a graphical, real-time illustration of the computer's CPU and physical memory usage. Click the Resource Monitor button to get an expanded look at what's currently happening on your PC.

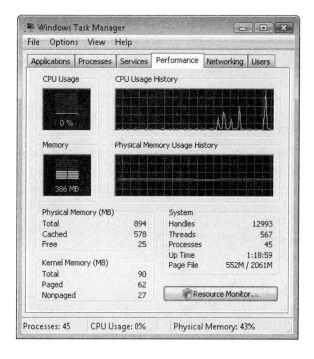

System Information

System Information is also a good tool to gather performance information about your computer. This doesn't help you solve any problems, but it gives you a good summary of all of the resources on your computer. You can then expand Hardware Resources, Components, or Software Environment to take a closer look at these individual components.

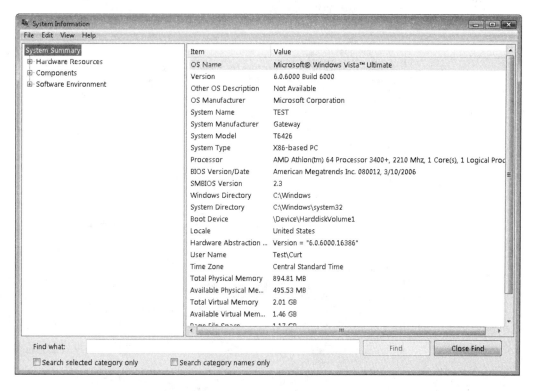

Appearance And Performance

The Appearance And Performance tool simply takes you back to the Performance Options dialog box we explored earlier in this project. Refer back to Step 3 for more information.

Disk Defragmenter

Disk fragmentation occurs over time as data is written to and deleted from your hard drive. Files can get fragmented, and as a result, it takes longer for Windows to read and write data to the disk. The Disk Defragmenter tool in Windows Vista is designed to help reduce fragmentation and is probably configured to run automatically every so often. You can access the tool here and run a defragmentation routine manually or adjust the automatic schedule.

System Health Report

The System Health Report is a cool feature of Windows Vista, providing you with information about hardware resources, system response times, and other processes. When you click the tool, it will collect the necessary data from your PC and create a report, which can then be used for troubleshooting purposes.

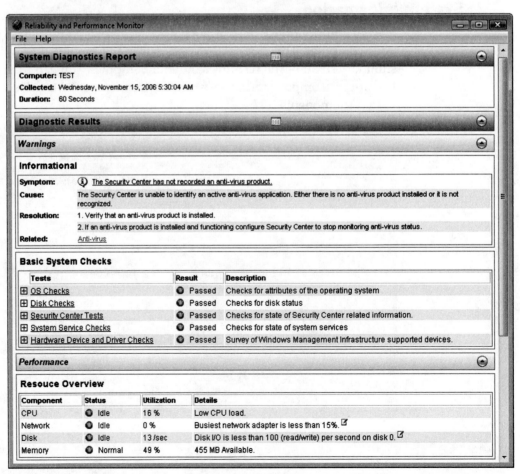

You might consider running this tool periodically to get an overall look at the health of your PC, and you should especially run this tool if your computer seems to be having performance problems. It can give you some clues that may help you troubleshoot the problem. The illustration shows you an example report.

Project 19

Use Windows Media Player at Your Next Party

What You'll Need

- Windows Vista: Any version
- Cost: Free

Windows Media Player is certainly nothing new in Windows Vista: It has been around since the days of the dinosaurs—at least, that's what it feels like. Media Player started out as a simple utility that played music and then developed into an overly bloated software package that was often frustrating and confusing. In Windows Vista, Media Player is better organized and easier to work with, which is good news for everyone. You can listen to music, watch movies, and even view photos. You can rip and burn music, sync with portable music devices, and access content online. However, in addition to all of those activities, you can use Media Player in a full-screen mode with a lock in place so that you can listen to music, see visualizations, and prevent anyone from directly accessing your computer. These features make Media Player a great tool to use at your next party, where you can use your PC to provide music but still keep curious eyes out of your operating system. In this project, you'll see how to use Media Player as an effective "stereo" for your next party.

Step 1: Plan Your Music

The first step to using Media Player at your next party begins not at your computer, but in your brain. You'll first need to decide what music you want to use for the party and how much you'll need. My wife and I have a Christmas party every year that typically lasts a few hours. It's a more formal event, where we like to have a lot of instrumental, classical music selections playing in the background. On the other hand, when my daughter has a party, she prefers rock 'n' roll. Whatever the case may be, you'll need to decide what music you want and how many songs you think you'll need for the party. You can have Media Player shuffle the songs and even replay them, but as a general rule, you should have a good selection of songs so that the music isn't repetitive.

Now you may have many of these songs already copied to the Media Library in Media Player, or perhaps they are scattered around on various CDs. Whatever the case may be, you'll need to gather up that music and all of the CDs you might need to copy the music from in order to create a playlist in Media Player. You can then have Media Player play, shuffle, and even repeat this playlist throughout the duration of the party. So plan what music you want, gather it up, and move on to Step 2.

Step 2: Rip Music from CDs

If you need to rip music from CDs so that Media Player can use it, you need to do that next. If your music is already copied to the Media Library, you can skip this step.

To rip music from a CD, put the CD into the CD drive and open Media Player. Click the Rip tab, and you'll see the album name and song titles listed, assuming you're connected to the Internet (shown in Figure 19-1). By default, all of the songs on the album are selected, but if there are songs you don't want to rip, simply clear the check box next to the song. When you're ready, click the Start Rip button. The songs will be copied to the Media Library. Repeat this process until you have copied all of the content from the different CDs that you want to use.

Figure 19-1

Rip music from your CDs.

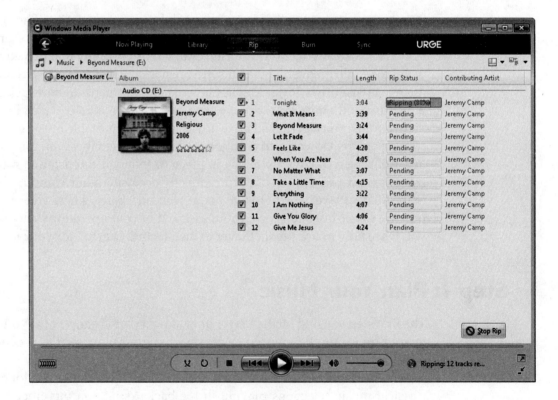

Step 3: Create a Playlist

Now that you have ripped music to the Media Library, you can create the playlist for your party. To create the playlist:

1. In Media Player, click the Library tab.

2. In the list on the left, expand the Playlists option, and click Create Playlist, shown in the following illustration. Type a name for the playlist, and press ENTER. You now have a new playlist in the Playlists category.

3. Now click the Library option to expand it, and then click the desired category. Since I have copied many songs from CDs, I'll choose the Album category to see the display of albums, as shown in the following illustration.

4. Double-click the desired album to see the song list. Then drag the songs you want to the playlist pane on the right side of the window. If you want to add all of the songs from the album on the playlist, drag the entire album to the window. Repeat this process until you have added all of the desired songs or albums to the playlist.

5. As the following illustration shows, you will see a listing of all current songs on the playlist. Notice that the playlist tells you how many songs it contains and approximately how long the playlist is in terms of playback time. If you decide you want to remove some of the songs from the playlist, right-click the song and click Remove From List.

6. When you're done, click the Save Playlist button to save it.

Step 4: Choose a Visualization

Before you use your playlist for your party in full-screen mode, you should select a visualization pattern that you like. A visualization is a graphic motion feature that will keep your computer from having a boring, blank screen during playback. Click the drop-down arrow under Now Playing in the Media Player, and point to Visualizations. As shown in Figure 19-2, you can choose no visualization, album art, or you can access additional sub-menus and choose visualization. You can click the ones that sound interesting and see how they look. You can also click the Download Visualizations option to access more visualizations on Microsoft's Web site.

Figure 19-2

Choose a visualization.

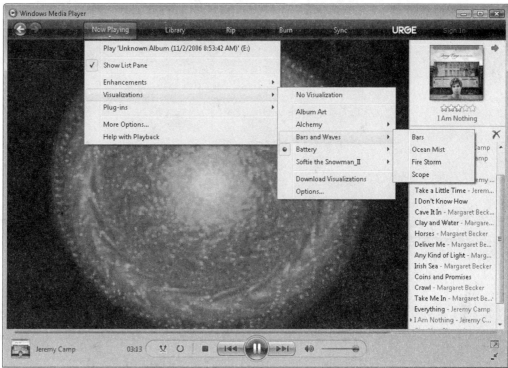

tip   *You must have music currently playing in the Now Playing area in order to see the visualization at work.*

Step 5: Go to Full-Screen Mode

When you're ready to use your playlist at a party, you just need to start playing the playlist, and then switch to full-screen mode. In the Media Library, select your playlist and click the Play button. Click the Now Playing button to make sure you are happy with the visualization you selected, and then click the View Full Screen button in the lower-right corner.

Media Player switches to full-screen mode, as you can see in Figure 19-3. Notice that you have the standard controls at the bottom of the screen. However, these will disappear after a moment, showing only the visualization. Use the controls to turn on shuffle if you like. Once the controls vanish, you can always see them again by moving the mouse to the bottom of the screen.

Step 6: Lock Full-Screen Mode

As it stands, you can use the full-screen mode for a party, but anyone who has access to your computer can leave full-screen mode and then have full access to your system. You can prevent this risk by locking the full-screen mode so that a code must be entered in order to leave full screen.

Figure 19-3

Full-screen mode

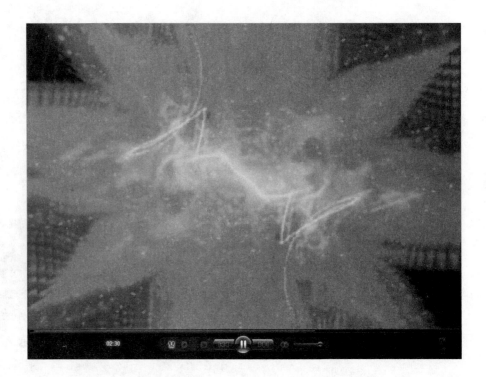

Turn on the full-screen mode lock by clicking the Lock button on the control bar when you're in full-screen mode. The Lock button is found on the lower-right portion of the control bar. Click the Lock button, and type a four-digit PIN number, as shown in Figure 19-4. The Lock button changes to a check box. Click it to enable the lock. In order to exit full-screen mode, you must click the lock again and enter the PIN number. Should you forget the PIN number, you'll need to restart the computer.

Figure 19-4

Click the Lock button and enter a PIN number.

Solve Home Network Connection Problems

What You'll Need

- **Windows Vista: Any version**
- **Cost: Free**

Home networking has been a great advancement in the PC world. Since most households now have more than one computer, often with the need to share a wireless Internet connection and peripherals, home networking has become more popular and more necessary.

Of course, in the past, home networking was a major pain. You had to know a great deal about Transmission Control Protocol/Internet Protocol (TCP/IP) settings, and when you had a connection problem, solving it was often difficult—if not impossible—without professional help. Great news—Windows Vista makes home networking and trouble-shooting home networks much easier than it has been in the past, and there are some new tools available that you might overlook if you're not careful. In this project, I'll show you the steps you should take and tools you can put to work in Windows Vista that will help you get your home network up and running in no time.

Step 1: Check the Network Map

Windows Vista includes a new feature called "network map." In many cases, a connection problem can be found more quickly if you look at a graphical representation of your network. It can help you see where the connection problems may be taking place.

To access the network map, open the Network And Sharing Center in Control Panel. As you can see in the Network And Sharing Center, there is a quick network map view, along with other information about your network, shown in Figure 20-1.

Figure 20-1

Network and
Sharing Center

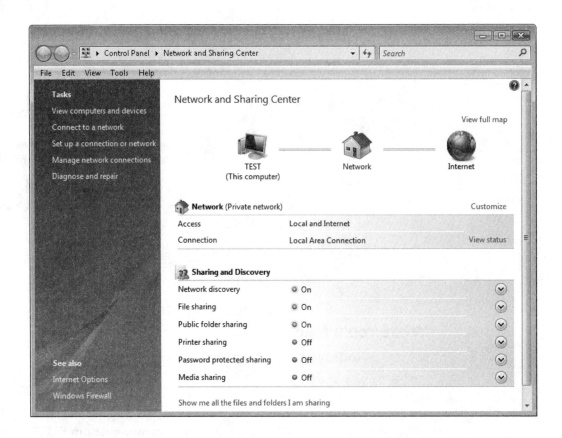

<table>
<tr><td>

Tasks

View computers and devices

Connect to a network

Set up a connection or network

Manage network connections

Diagnose and repair

</td></tr>
</table>

It may sound elementary, but always check your connection cables on the network when you
have problems. I know of many instances where individuals spent hours trying to figure out a
network connection problem when the only problem was that a cable to a device or computer
had become unplugged. You never know what your children (or cat or dog) may have done, so
check the cables first!

If you click the View Full Map option, an additional window opens, displaying the
map shown in Figure 20-2. If you click the different items on the network map, Windows Vista will attempt to connect to them. You can also click the View Computers And
Devices link in the left pane to get a look at the individual items on your network.

In order for network map to be displayed, the Network Discovery feature must be turned on.
Go back to the Network And Sharing Center, and under Sharing and Discovery, make sure that
Network Discovery is activated.

Step 2: Have Windows Vista Diagnose and Repair the Network Problem

If there are connection problems on the network, it could be that your computer or
another computer has some kind of network setting that is preventing it from connecting. For example, a TCP/IP setting or a firewall setting could be causing the
problem. Fortunately, Windows Vista can detect these kinds of problems and often

Figure 20-2

Network map

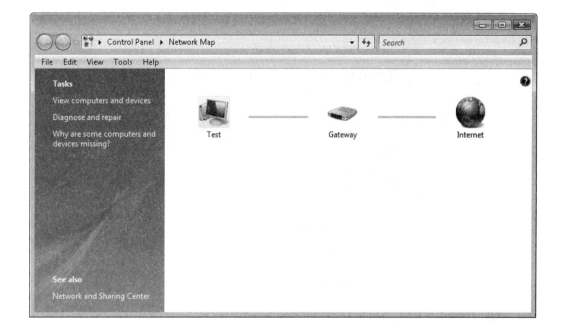

automatically repair them. If you open the Network And Sharing Center, notice the Diagnose And Repair option in the left pane. Simply click this option and Windows Vista will detect and attempt to repair any problems, as you can see in Figure 20-3. Once Windows Vista attempts to detect and fix the problem, it will tell you what, if any, problems were found and what has been fixed.

Figure 20-3

Windows Vista can diagnose and repair many network connection problems.

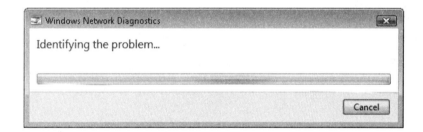

Step 3: Check the Status of a Connection

You can gather more information about the status of a connection by accessing a connection's properties. This can often help you troubleshoot networking problems. Open the Network And Sharing Center, and then click Manage Network Connections in the Tasks pane. In the Network Connections folder, shown in Figure 20-4, you see icons for any network connections that your computer has. When you select a connection icon, you have toolbar options, enabling you to disable the network device (which disables your computer's network adapter card), diagnose the connection, rename the connection, view the status of the connection, or change the settings of the connection. Click View Status Of This Connection, or you can just double-click the icon.

Figure 20-4

Network connections

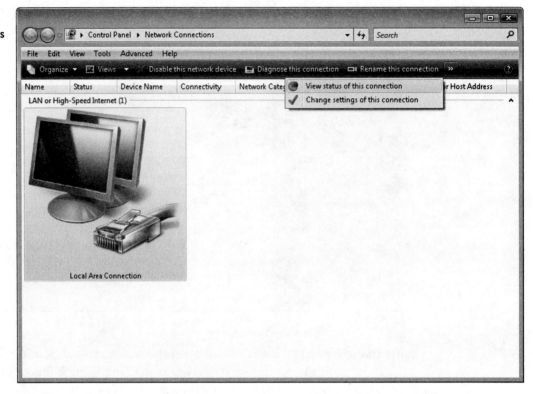

The Local Area Connection status dialog box appears, shown in Figure 20-5. The status information gives you data about the connection, provided the connection is working. If it isn't, check the Media State option and make sure that it says "Enabled."

Figure 20-5

Local area connection status

If you click the Details button, you'll see more information about the network connection, shown in the following illustration. This will tell you about the TCP/IP addressing and other settings. If you need to call technical support for help, the support technician will likely want information from this dialog box.

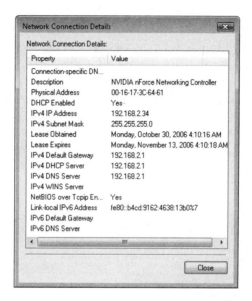

Also notice on the Local Area Connection Status dialog box (see Figure 20-5) that you can access the properties of the local area connection, disable it, or again access the diagnose option. If you click the Properties button, you will see more detailed information about the network services and protocols that are at work for this connection, shown in the following illustration. The options that you see here are configured when you first set up your network and typically do not need direct intervention from you. However, in some cases, you may need to access the properties for these different services and protocols or install others. You should get the help of a networking professional before you attempt to make manual changes to the options you see here.

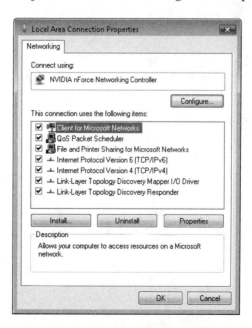

Step 4: Check the Sharing and Discovery Settings

When your network is set up, Windows Vista turns on certain settings automatically, depending on the kind of network you are connecting to. Typically, network discovery, file sharing, and public folder sharing is turned on for private networks. You can check these settings to make sure everything is turned on so that you have connectivity.

If you open the Network And Sharing Center, you can click the expansion arrow next to any one of these items to see details about it. As you can see in Figure 20-6, I have expanded the Network Discovery option. I can see that Network Discovery is turned on, and I can even access Windows Vista Help to learn more about this feature. I can do the same thing for the other sharing options available here, and I can turn them on, too. For example, if I want to start sharing a printer on the network, I can expand the Printer Sharing option and turn on the feature.

Figure 20-6

Network Discovery
Option

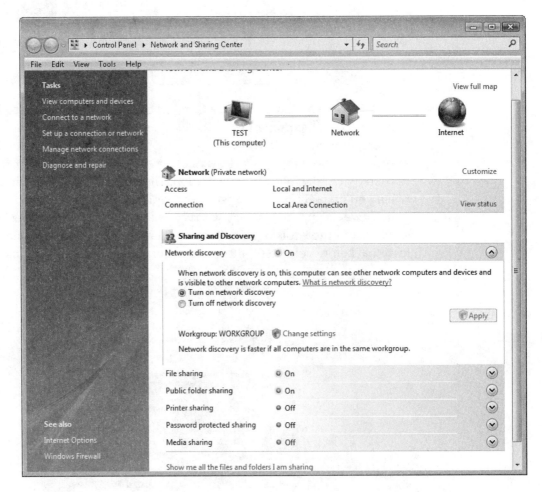

Step 5: Make Sure Your Computer Is Connected to the Correct Network

In some cases—especially where your computer is used to connect to different networks, such as a laptop with a wireless connection—the connection problem may simply be that Windows Vista is trying to connect to the wrong network. You can check and correct this problem quickly and easily. Open the Network Sharing Center in Control Panel, and click the Connect To A Network option in the Tasks pane. In the Connect To A Network dialog box that appears, Windows Vista will tell you if there is a different network available that you can connect to. In Figure 20-7, Windows Vista did not find an additional network, but if it had, I would see it listed here and the Connect button would be enabled so that I could connect to it.

Figure 20-7

Connect to another network.

Project 21

Make Your Important Data Automatically Save Itself

What You'll Need

- Windows Vista: Any version
- Cost: Free

You know the sad story. Maybe you've even experienced it yourself. You spent hours working on a collection of documents—maybe you even stayed up all night. And the next morning, your PC has a meltdown. Maybe the hard drive has become fried egg or the motherboard now looks like toast. No matter what the issue, you get the sinking feeling that all your hard work is lost.

Unfortunately, this sad story is all too true—it happens to computer users every day, and although you've heard over and over that you should back up your data, most of us don't take the time on a day-to-day basis to make sure our data is backed up and secure. In an age where everything, including photos and family video, is stored on the computer, backing up data is more important now than ever before.

In the past, backing up data was a bit difficult. You had to know some technical terms and ideas to do it really well, but in Windows Vista, it is much easier to back up your data. In fact, you can even have Windows Vista do it automatically for you. In this project, you'll see how to back up your data and how to automate this critical task.

Step I: Get Ready to Back Up Data

You can back up data in a number of ways: You can save data to a CD, DVD, a removable disk drive, an external disk drive, or even another computer on a local network. You can manually save the files you want; should a problem ever occur, you will still have your data. However, backing up important information this way is time-consuming and heavily dependent on you. Why not let Windows Vista automatically handle this task for you?

To help you accomplish your backup goals, Windows Vista gives you the Backup And Restore Center, which provides a number of different backup options.

Click Start | Control Panel | Backup And Restore Center. The interface, shown in Figure 21-1, gives you the choice between backing up files or backing up the entire computer. You can also access the Backup And Restore Center to restore certain files or restore your entire computer.

Figure 21-1

Backup And Restore Center

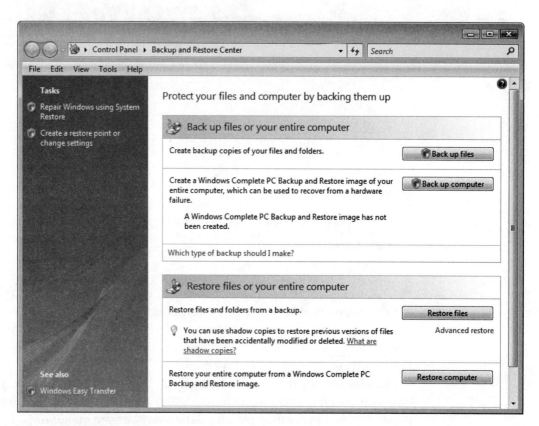

Certainly, you should perform a complete backup of your computer in the event of a hard drive failure, but most of the time, you'll be more concerned with backing up files. In the next step, you'll run the Backup utility for the first time.

Step 2: Run the Backup Wizard

The following procedure explains how to use the Backup Wizard and will explain the options available to you.

1. Click Start | Control Panel | Backup And Restore Center.

2. The Backup And Restore Center appears. There are two basic sections in this interface. You can create a backup of files and folders of your choice or you can use Complete PC Backup to copy the entire hard drive. This gives you an "image" that you can use to restore your computer fully in the event of

a hardware failure, such as a disk drive crash. You can make copies of your files and folders by clicking the Backup Files button.

3. On the Backup Or Restore window, choose the location where you want to save your backup, such as your local computer, DVD, or even on the network, shown in Figure 21-2. Make your selection and click Next.

Figure 21-2

Choose a backup location.

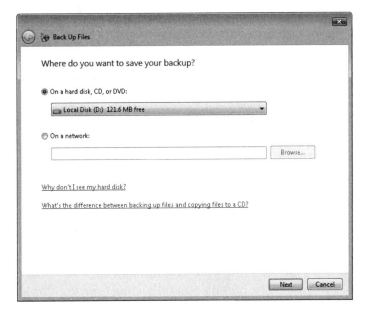

4. In the next window, you can choose the kind of files that you want to back up. Select the kinds of files you want by selecting the check boxes. Clear the check boxes for the kinds of files you don't want to back up, shown in Figure 21-3. Click Next.

Figure 21-3

Choose the kinds of files you want to back up.

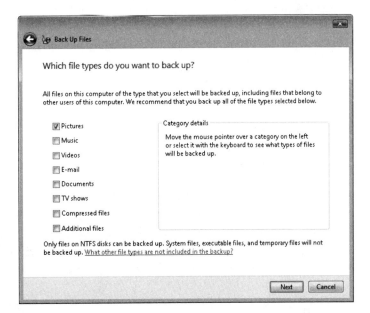

5. In the next window, choose how often you want to back up these files by clicking the drop-down menu for each category. How often you back up data depends on your computer use. The more you create and edit files, the more often you should back up. For most home users, once a week is typically a good choice. When you're done, click the Save Settings And Start Backup button.

 Keep in mind that the options you select here create a backup schedule. You may want to have the backup run early in the morning or late at night or on certain days of the week. Just think about your needs and how often you change or create new data to determine how often you should back up.

Step 2: Back Up Your Entire PC

If you want to back up everything on your computer so that your operating system and all data can be restored in the event of hardware failure, you'll use the Complete PC option.

1. In the Backup And Restore Center, click the Back Up Computer button.

2. In the next window, you can choose to back up the image to your computer or to one or more DVDs. If you choose the hard disk option, your disk must be formatted with New Technology File System (NTFS). Click Next.

3. Confirm your settings and click the Save Settings And Start Backup button. The backup will take some time to complete, possibly several hours.

Step 3: Making Changes to Your Backup Schedule

So you've created a backup schedule so that your files are backed up often to prevent loss. However, what if you need to change that schedule? Windows Vista gives you a quick and easy tool to alter the backup schedule if necessary.

Click Start | All Programs | Accessories | System Tools | Backup Status And Configuration. As you can see in Figure 21-4, this simple interface gives you information about the last backup and enables you to manually override the backup schedule by clicking the Backup Now option. You can also click the Change Backup Settings link to adjust the backup schedule as necessary.

Step 4: Restore Your Data

Just as you can back up your data, you can use the Backup And Restore Center to restore data to your computer. You can choose to use the File And Folder Restore Wizard to restore lost files and folders from a backup. You can also use the Shadow Copies feature to restore previous versions of files that have been accidentally deleted or modified. For example, let's say that you're working on the great American novel, and you accidentally delete some sections you didn't intent to. Windows Vista keeps previous versions of files and folders, which are saved as a "restore point." Any file

Figure 21-4

Backup status
and configuration

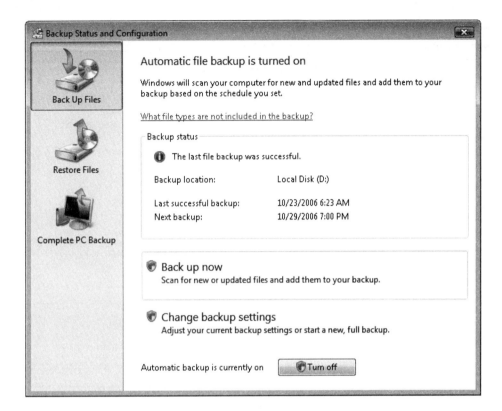

or folder that was modified since the last restore point was made—which is typically 24 hours earlier—is saved and made available as a previous version. You can then restore the file from the previous version that was saved, which is called a "shadow copy." You can find out more about working with shadow copies in Project 22.

To restore lost data:

1. Click Start | Control Panel | Backup And Restore.

2. Click the Restore Files button.

3. In the Restore Wizard, choose to restore files from the latest backup, and click Next.

4. In the next window, you can choose to restore everything in the backup, or you can restore certain files or folders by browsing for them (see Figure 21-5). If you have made an accidental deletion within a file or folder, use the Browse feature to locate it. This is where Windows Vista will use the Shadow Copies feature to restore the file or folder. Click Next.

5. You can choose to restore files and folders to their original locations, or you can specify a new location. Make your selection and click the Start Restore button.

In the event that your computer is greatly damaged and you want to do a complete restore, assuming you backed up your computer using the Complete PC Backup

Figure 21-5

Choose what you
want to restore.

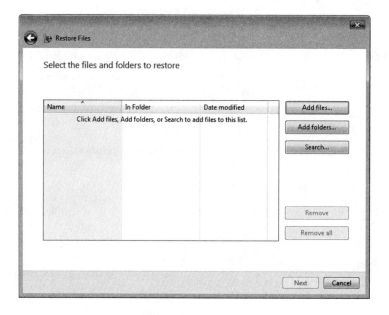

feature, just click the Restore Computer button. This process will completely reformat your disks and overwrite all existing data on your computer, so you only want to use this option when absolutely necessary. When you click the Restore Computer option, you'll see a warning message and also instructions (see Figure 21-6) telling you to shut down the computer and restart it using the Windows Recovery Environment by holding down the F8 key during startup. Once you access the Windows Recovery Environment, choose Windows Complete PC Backup, and follow the instructions that appear.

Figure 21-6

Warning message

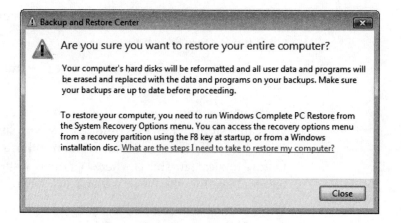

Retrieve a Lost File with Shadow Copy

What You'll Need

- **Windows Vista: Any version**
- **Cost: Free**

It's happened to everyone who has ever used a computer. Something goes wrong, a mistake is made, and that really important file for work or letter you've written to a friend gets damaged or completely deleted from your computer. In the past, you were really out of luck. Perhaps a third-party deletion recovery utility could help, or if you were wise enough (and took the time) to actually back up your files, you could get it back that way. But for most of us, the file was toast and we had to start from scratch.

Good news: Windows Vista provides a new feature called Shadow Copy, which, in most cases, will give you the power to fix a corrupted file or recover a file that you have accidentally deleted. Shadow Copy works automatically—all you have to do is put this easily missed but important feature of Windows Vista to work.

Step 1: Understanding "Previous Versions" and "Shadow Copies"

In order to get the most out of the Shadow Copies feature, you have to understand the concept of "previous versions" in Windows Vista and System Restore. Once you understand these concepts, shadow copies will make better sense to you and you'll know when and how to use them.

In Windows Vista, previous versions of files and folders are either backup copies that you have backed up using the Backup utility or they are shadow copies, which are made as a part of the System Restore process in Windows Vista. As such, you can use previous versions to restore an accidentally modified or deleted file, or you can restore that file from backup. Of course, if you had the backup file, you probably wouldn't care about shadow copies. Shadow copies work best when there is no previous version to restore from backup.

Shadow copies of your files are automatically saved as part of a restore point for System Restore. By default, your computer automatically creates "restore points" periodically, which enables the computer to restore your files, folders, and personal data in the event of a system failure or problem. Windows Vista automatically creates restore points if the System Protection feature is turned on. You can check this by opening the System applet in Control Panel. In the left pane, click System Protection. On the System Protection tab, shown in Figure 22-1, you can see the disk that is being protected and when the most recent restore point was created.

Figure 22-1

The System
Protection feature

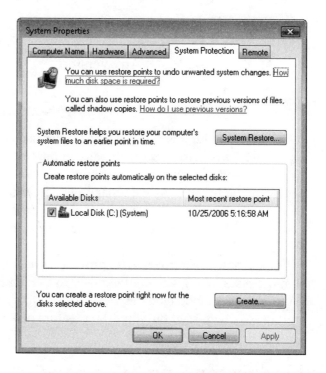

> **tip** Let's say you are about to work on several files on your computer. If you want to be really safe, you can manually create a restore point before you begin. Should something happen, you'll have a recent restore point to restore from. On the System Protection tab, click the Create button, give the new restore point a name, and click OK. A new, current restore point will be created.

In case you're wondering, restore points are created every day and just before "significant" events, such as software or driver installation. So shadow copies of your files are created at least once a day. In the event of damage or deletion, you can retrieve the file from the shadow copy so that you will at least have a previous version. Naturally, not all changes may be available in the file, depending on when the last shadow copy was made, but you can least recover the file from 24 hours ago.

Step 2: Accessing a Previous Version

Let's say you have a file or folder where something has changed—but not for the better. The first thing you need to do is access the Previous Versions feature on the file or folder's properties page so you can see if a previous version exists.

Right-click the file or folder, and click Restore Previous Versions. On the Previous Versions tab, you can see if earlier versions of the file or folder exist. For example, in Figure 22-2, I have a previous version of a particular file that is two days old (it was shadow-copied on October 23 and today is October 25).

Figure 22-2

The Previous Versions feature shows you what shadow copies are available.

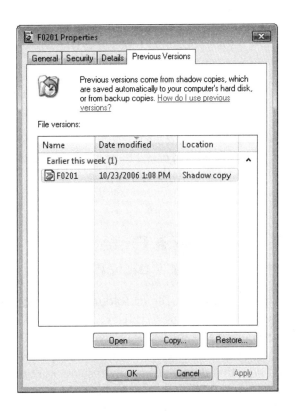

note *Shadow copies are made of your files and folders locally and on a network, provided one is available. However, it is possible for a network administrator to disable the feature for network files. Also, shadow copies do not exist for files and folders that Windows needs to function properly, such as the files and folders that are typically stored in C:\Windows. In the event that something goes wrong with your computer, simply run System Restore and allow Windows to replace its own files that could be causing the problem. This is not something you can manually do with shadow copies (or would even want to anyway, since Windows Vista can do the work for you).*

Step 3: Restore a Shadow Copy

If you need to restore a file or folder using a shadow copy, you can easily do so from the Restore Previous Versions tab. Simply right-click the file or folder you want to restore, and click Restore Previous Versions. On the tab (see Figure 22-2), select the version you want to restore, and click the Restore button. Before you click Restore, however, understand that this process will delete any current version of the file and replace it with the older version. This process cannot be undone either. The moral of the story is to make sure you want to restore the file before doing so. Once you click Restore, you'll see a confirmation dialog box, shown in the following illustration. Click Restore again to continue.

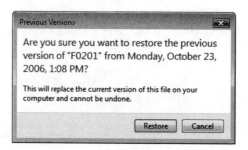

note   When you access the Previous Versions feature, you'll see the file or folder from the shadow copy, but you'll also see it listed here if there is a backup copy of it as well. If you choose to restore the backup copy, the Restore Files Wizard will guide you through the process.

Step 4: Recovering a Deleted or Renamed File or Folder

In the event that a file or folder has been completely deleted from your computer, you may still be able to retrieve it using a shadow copy. To do so, you need to know the location that the file was saved to. For example, let's say that you have file named Siamese Cats. You saved that file to a folder in Documents called Cats. You would need to know that the file originally resided in the Cats folder to get it back; otherwise, you won't know where to look for the recent version.

To recover the deleted or renamed file or folder, open Documents and use the Folders list to navigate to the folder that held the lost file or folder, right-click it, and click Restore Previous Versions. Look through the Previous Versions list, and locate the item that was deleted or renamed. Once you've found it, you can drag the file or folder to another location, such as your desktop, and the file or folder will be saved to that new location. You can then use it as you normally would.

Build a Custom DVD

What You'll Need

- Windows Vista: Any version
- DVD-R disc
- Cost: $2 or less

I've been making custom DVDs for years, and I love it. Every time we have a family vacation or a holiday, my friends and family expect me to make a DVD with photos and video from the event—and, of course, they expect me to send them a copy. I don't mind—there is something about editing video footage and compiling photos with music in the background that I find both relaxing and creatively satisfying. However, I've been building those products for years on a Macintosh.

Finally, Microsoft steps up to the plate with a good DVD maker, which you can find in Windows Vista. It works well, is generally easy to use once you get the hang of it, and it enables you to customize your DVD in a way that you want. The good news is you can get started with something easy and then move on to more complicated projects as you get the hang of the software. In this project, I'll show you how to make a custom DVD.

Step 1: Build Your Movie in Windows Movie Maker

Windows DVD Maker is essentially an assembly and burner package. It doesn't build movies. Although you can create a custom slide show using photos from within DVD Maker, if you plan on using video footage, you need to edit it and assemble your movie using Windows Movie Maker. You then use Windows DVD Maker to put that movie on a customized DVD. Project 12 in this book shows you how to use Windows Movie Maker to create a movie, so you might want to check out that project before moving forward.

Step 2: Get Ready to Use the DVD Maker

You can open Windows DVD Maker by clicking Start | Programs | Windows DVD Maker. When you first open Windows DVD Maker, you see a basic interface with no content, as shown in Figure 23-1.

Figure 23-1

Windows DVD Maker

Before using DVD Maker, you may want to change one of the options that determines how DVD Maker works. Notice the Options link in the lower-right corner. Click this link to open the DVD Options dialog box, shown in Figure 23-2. You can choose how your DVD is played back. You have the option to start with a DVD menu

Figure 23-2

DVD options

(this is the default), play video and end with a DVD menu, or play video in a continuous loop. In most cases, starting with a menu is the easiest way to use a DVD, and it is the standard DVD format you're probably already used to anyway. You don't need to change the DVD aspect ratio or video format. When you're done, click OK.

Step 3: Add Content

The first thing you need to do is add media items to your DVD. If you're using a movie you created with Windows Movie Maker, just click DVD under Publish, and your movie will be sent to Windows DVD Maker. Figure 23-3 shows you an example of a Windows Movie Maker movie added directly to Windows DVD Maker.

However, you can also add other items, or you can mix video and photos from scratch as well. Click the Add Items button on the toolbar. This opens a standard folder interface, where you can browse for your movies, video clips, or photos. Windows DVD Maker can read and use most standard file formats. Locate and select your items, and click the Open button, shown in Figure 23-4. Remember that you can select multiple items at the same time by holding down the CTRL key and selecting the items you want.

The new items will appear in DVD Maker. If you choose photos, they will be placed in a folder called Slide Show within the DVD Maker interface, as you can see in Figure 23-5. You can double-click the folder to see the photos. When you're done, click the Back To Videos button on the toolbar.

Figure 23-3

Windows Movie Maker movie in DVD Maker

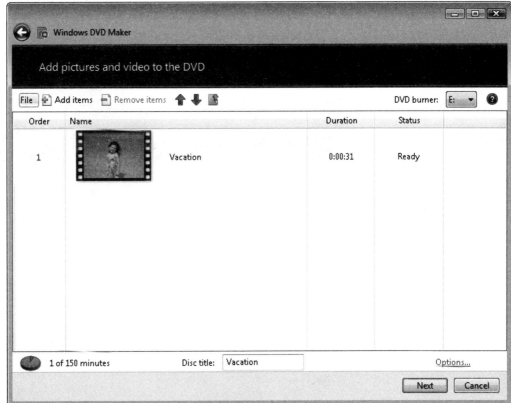

Figure 23-4

Select the desired
items and click Open.

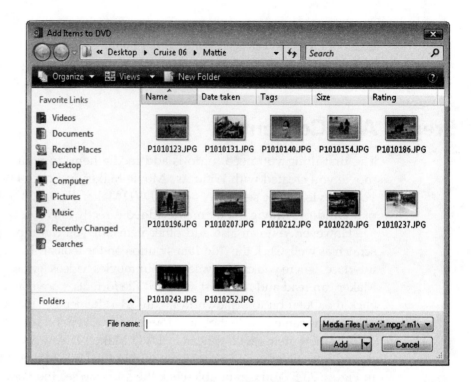

As you're adding items, notice that you can use the toolbar buttons to remove items, or you can select an item and move it up or down in the list. Make sure the order of the items is as you want, because the order you see here is the order for the DVD. If you're using a slide show and you want to change the order of the photos, double-click the folder to see the photos. Then use the Move Up or Move Down button to reorder the photos. When you're done, just click Back To Videos.

Figure 23-5

Photos appear in
a folder called Slide
Show.

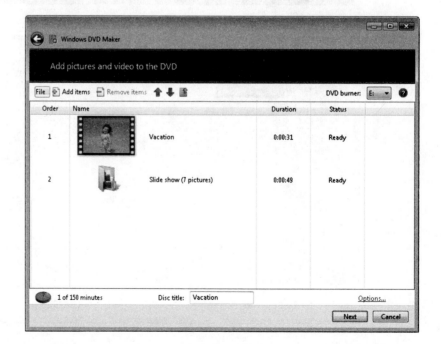

Before moving forward, notice that there is a Disc Title text box toward the bottom of the window. By default, the title is set to today's date. However, you can change the title to whatever you want.

Now that everything is added and ordered the way you want, click Next and read on.

Step 4: Configure the Menu

In the next window, you'll see the option to burn your disc. However, before doing so, you have some additional options that you need to configure. The first is the DVD menu, which is what you'll see when you put the DVD into a DVD player. To create a menu:

1. In the Menu Styles pane on the right, click through the menu items to locate the one that you want. When you click a menu style, you can see it in the interface. Notice that the menus will use pieces of your DVD content, as shown in Figure 23-6.

Figure 23-6

Choose a menu format.

2. You may want to change some things about the menu, and you can easily do so. First, click the Menu Text button on the toolbar. Choose the Font option, and then adjust the labels for the disc title, Play button, Scenes button, and Notes button (if desired). Once you make your changes, you can click the Preview button to see your changes (see Figure 23-7). Click Save when you're done.

Figure 23-7

Change the font and labels for the DVD menu.

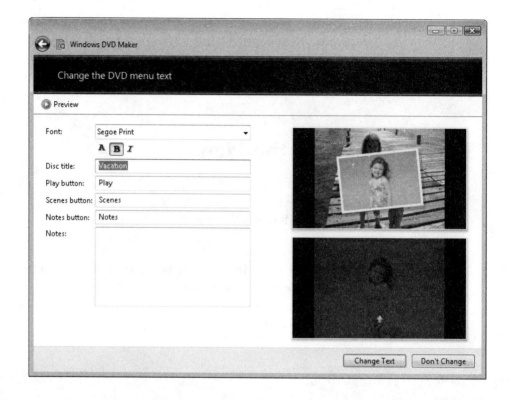

3. Now click the Customize Menu button on the toolbar. You can use the text boxes and buttons to adjust the foreground and background video, menu audio, motion menu, and scene buttons, shown in Figure 23-8. The video

Figure 23-8

Customize the DVD menu.

options allow you to pull in other videos or photos to use within the menu so that the movie looks the way you want it. Make any desired changes here, and click Save.

Step 5: Configuring Your Slide Show

If your DVD includes a folder of photos for a slide show, you can click the Slide Show button on the toolbar and make some adjustments as to how the slide show looks when it is played. You'll see a window, shown in Figure 23-9, where you have the following options:

- **Music**   Use the Add Music button to add music stored on your computer or a device connected to your computer to the slide show. You'll see a standard Open dialog box, where you can browse and select the music you want.

- **Slide show length**   You can change the slide show length to match the music clip you're using. You can also change the picture length so that each photo is displayed for a certain number of seconds. Typically, 7 to 10 seconds is enough.

- **Transition**   You can choose a transition between the photos. Use the drop-down menu to make your selection. The transition you choose applies to all photos. In other words, you can't assign different transitions to different photos.

- **Pan and zoom**   You can use these features so that your photos appear to have movement.

Figure 23-9

Choose the slide show settings, and click Save.

Step 6: Previewing Your DVD

Now that you have your settings and content configured, click the Preview button on the toolbar to see a preview of your DVD (see Figure 23-10). After the preview, you'll still be able to make changes to the menu and slide show if necessary. When you click Preview, DVD Maker will generate the move and begin playing it from the menu. Use the standard controls on the interface to view your movie.

Figure 23-10

Preview your DVD.

Step 7: Burn Your DVD

When you have finished previewing your movie and you have made any final changes, you are ready to burn your DVD. Make sure you are happy with your DVD before burning it because you cannot stop the burn process to make changes. When you're ready, click Start Burn. The interface disappears and you see a Burning dialog box. The burning process will take some time—it will take longer if your content is long. When the process is complete, you now have a DVD that will play on any standard DVD player!

Turn Your PC into a GPS Device

What You'll Need

- Windows Vista: Any version
- GPS hardware and/or software
- Cost: $150 or less

Ever feel lost? No, I'm not talking philosophically—I'm talking about really lost. You're in a city and you can't find your way around, a road trip goes amuck, or maybe you just want the power to track places and events on your Windows Vista computer.

No matter what the case may be, there is a solution with a global positioning system (GPS). GPS technology allows your computer to interact with both software and hardware to receive GPS data, or at least it can interact with an Internet server that does. You can even connect a GPS device to your laptop and use it when you're traveling to help you find your way.

Whatever your needs may be, there is a GPS solution that will work for you, and in this project, we'll explore your possibilities.

Step 1: Simple Software Solutions

There are several different ways you can use GPS, one of which is as a software solution. Naturally, software solutions typically require an Internet connection. You use the software, which interacts with an Internet server that uses GPS, to locate what you want. In this section, I'll introduce you to some of the software solutions you may enjoy.

Google Earth

A free software tool that is loads of fun and a great place to get started with GPS is Google Earth, which you can download from earth.google.com. Just download the software and install it. Then determine where you want to go around the planet. Fly in from outer space, if you will, and check out how things look in China or Egypt or wherever. You can have hours of fun with this tool. Figure 24-1 gives you a sample of Google Earth looking at the Golden Gate Bridge.

Figure 24-1

Google Earth

Topofusion

Another fun tool you can try for free is Topofusion. This GPS mapping software shows you topological and aerial maps that can be downloaded on demand. You can try the free version to get a feel for the software or purchase it for $40. Visit www.topofusion .com to learn more. Figure 24-2 gives you an idea of what's available.

Live Local

As a part of Windows Live, you can access Live Local and get Virtual Earth 3D, which is a similar 3D mapping and viewing program. As with Google Earth, this software is loads of fun and it's all free, which is also nice. Figure 24-3 shows you a sample.

Microsoft Streets And Trips

Aside from basic GPS mapping software packages, you can also find a plethora of GPS locator software packages for PCs, laptops, mobile devices, and smart phones.

Figure 24-2

Topofusion

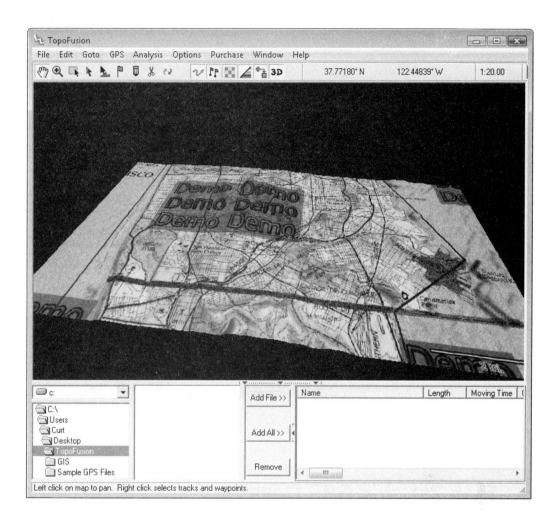

Naturally, there are too many to mention in this project, but there are a couple of popular packages I want to point out. The first is Microsoft Streets And Trips, which can be purchased at any software store for around $70.

Streets And Trips is trip-planning software that comes with a Universal Serial Bus (USB) GPS receiver that you can attach to your computer (learn more about GPS receivers in Step 2). It can give you distance-based and voice-prompted directions, door-to-door driving directions, and boasts over 1.8 million points of interest in the U.S. and Canada. The software also works with MSN's Virtual Earth software if you want a quick bird's eye view of the area.

Delorme Earthmate GPS

Another software package designed to turn your laptop into a GPS tracking device is Delorme Earthmate. This software can show you your real-time position using the Street Atlas in the USA. You can also create address-to-address driving instructions and find more than 4 million places of interest. This package, which also comes with a GPS receiver, is around $90 at most computer software stores.

Figure 24-3

Virtual Earth 3D

Step 2: Using GPS Devices

If you're interested in a software/device solution that can allow you to track yourself while driving and even give you voice directions, Streets And Trips, as well as Earthmate, provide you with a USB GPS tracking device, but the reviews are rather mixed about how well they will help you get from one destination to the other. Naturally, these systems are less expensive, so depending on your needs, you might consider one of these devices and related software:

Garmin

Garmin makes a popular GPS device called StreetPilot (read more about it at www .garmin.com). StreetPilot is a high-sensitivity GPS receiver and device that comes ready to use right out of the box. It is essentially a navigator that gives you voice and display directions, but it also Bluetooth-enabled and even has an MP3 player built in. Figure 24-4 shows you a quick look at StreetPilot. You can purchase it for around $750. Naturally, this product is expensive, so if you're just getting into GPS devices, try out some of the less expensive products first.

Figure 24-4

StreetPilot

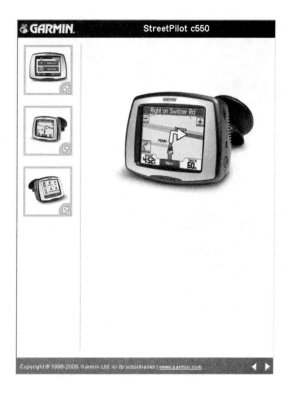

Magellan

Magellan is the GPS manufacturer that provides the RoadMate series of products, namely the eXplorist series and Magellan CrossoverGPS. The eXplorist device provides an outdoor GPS receiver and is compatible with MapSend topographic and street routing software. It's a great, portable GPS device that you can easily carry with you. The CrossoverGPS device looks more like a personal digital assistant (PDA) and works well in your car or if you're out hiking. At the time of this writing, the CrossoverGPS hasn't been released yet. Devices in the eXplorist series cost between $150-400, depending on the model you want. You can find out more at www.magellangps.com.

Navman

Navman makes in-car navigation and PDA devices for GPS navigation. These products provide many of the same features as the other products mentioned, but include photo navigation and an easy-to-view screen. Figure 24-5 shows you an example. You can find out more about the Navman products at www.navman.com.

Step 3: Installing GPS Software and Devices

Installing your GPS software and device, no matter what package you decide is right for you, is rather easy. For most packages, you simply install the software using the installation CD-ROM. Just insert the CD-ROM to start the installation, and follow

Figure 24-5

Navman N40i

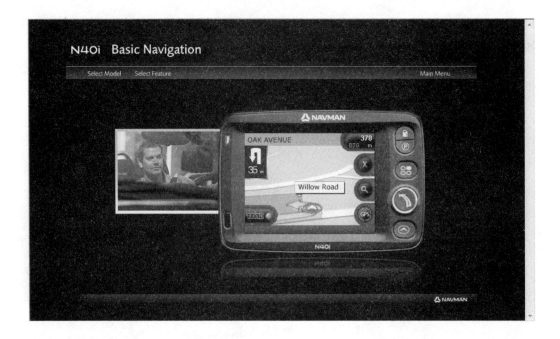

the prompts. Once installation is complete, most GPS devices attach to an available USB port on your computer. Since the installation of the software typically installs the GPS device drivers as well, there's usually nothing more you need to do than plug the device into your computer. Windows Vista will automatically detect and install the device so that it is ready and working on your computer.

Naturally, you need to make sure that any product you buy is compatible with Windows Vista. Although products designed for Windows XP will most likely work with Windows Vista, there is no guarantee they will, and you may be required to download an upgrade for the software. As with all software, it's best to try and purchase a product that states compatibility with Windows Vista right on the box.

Step 4: Putting It Altogether

As you have seen in this project, GPS navigation requires both software and hardware. You'll have to determine which solution is best for you. You can certainly choose a hardware device, as explored in the previous section, but pricing does play a factor.

With a laptop running Windows Vista and USB GPS software/device, you can have a lot of fun and find your way around for less than $100, so this solution is typically the best starting point. When you take your next road trip, simply bring the laptop and GPS device along and see how it can help you find your way as you travel.

As you can imagine, I've only showed you a few options in this project to get you interested. Ultimately, you need to make a decision about what product is right for you. With that in mind, be sure to visit www.gpsinformation.net, where you can read about all sorts of products and software. This site can help you narrow down which products will best meet your particular needs.

Index